RISE

Rise: Game-Changing Success Strategies for Women Leaders is a practical guide that highlights the competitive edge of inclusivity within a company. This book, written by Jackie Stallings Evans, is a game-changer! Readers will have the ability to gain insights into fostering an inclusive culture and discover effective strategies for leading multicultural teams across generations, cultures, and in remote/hybrid work settings. This book is a must-read for leaders committed to advancing their leadership skills to the next level.

Melonie Parker
Chief Diversity Officer, Google

Rise: Game-Changing Success Strategies for Women Leaders by Jackie Stallings Evans is a must-read for ALL aspiring executives as you navigate your way up the corporate ladder. It is a practical guidebook full of enlightening examples of how she overcame obstacles and enjoyed a very successful career at IBM. Among many nuggets, she describes the importance of agile leadership, establishing executive presence, how to avoid workplace burnout, and why you should give back to your community.

Wes Coleman
Former Executive Vice President
and Chief Human Resources Officer
The Walt Disney Company

Wouldn't it be wonderful if you knew exactly what to say and do when facing the up-and-down challenges that come with growing your reputation and career as a trusted leader? If so, you'll love the warm wisdom, real-life examples, and actionable insights of this page-turning book. Get ready to underline passages that will save you trial-and-terror learning. Read it and reap.

Sam Horn, CEO of The Intrigue Agency

Jackie provides an easy-to-follow (and even easier to implement) roadmap to develop your "leadership signature," leveraging your uniqueness, credibility, and self-efficacy. This is a must-read for anyone wanting to "rise."

Lisa S. Kaplowitz
Executive Director, Rutgers Center for Women in Business
Associate Professor of Professional Practice - Finance,
Rutgers Business School

This practical and insightful gift will benefit all who want to achieve their leadership potential and those committed to creating an inclusive and engaged culture.

Ann Van Eron, Ph.D. CEO of Potentials, author of *OASIS Conversations: Leading with an Open Mindset to Maximize Potential* and *Open Stance: Thriving Amid Differences and Uncertainty*

Jackie Stallings Evans has enlightened us with a concept called "Mountain Climbing Momentum" to help you identify and overcome obstacles while navigating the corporate landscape. This is a practical and engaging book with strategies that anyone can use and apply.

Margot James Copeland
Independent Board Director;
Former Chair and CEO KeyBank Foundation

Jackie Stallings Evans shares heartfelt anecdotes and transformative insights to help other women, especially women of color, as they embrace their leadership potential in the corporate world.

Deepa Purushothaman,
Author of *The First, The Few, The Only*

Rise: Game-Changing Success Strategies for Women Leaders is full of stories and advice that will benefit anyone who wants to advance in today's workplace. This insightful book helps women find their leadership path and be more powerful as inclusive and agile leaders.

Dawn S. Kirk
Executive Coach, Speaker, and Author

With *Rise: Game-Changing Success Strategies for Women Leaders,* Jackie Stallings Evans provides a powerful and proven step-by-step guide for any woman aspiring to advance in the workplace. The message is clear - if you prepare yourself to overcome common barriers, you can achieve your career goals and rise up the corporate ladder.

Gena Cox,
PhD, Organizational Psychologist,
Executive Coach, Speaker, Author

Jackie Stallings Evans' use of storytelling is so beautifully poignant in *Rise: Game-Changing Success Strategies for Women Leaders.* You will be immediately drawn in from the first chapter. Her experiences give you an insight into her leadership journey with applicable lessons to take forward. The book is a must-read for those looking to elevate their leadership to the next level.

Simone E. Morris, Inclusive Leadership Expert
and Executive Career Coach

A direct, practical guide that reflects Jackie's profound insights and actionable strategies for women aiming to ascend into leadership roles. Her straightforward approach to overcoming obstacles and seizing leadership opportunities with confidence and skill makes Rise not only informative but also a necessary tool to get to the next level. Everyone needs a Jackie to inspire and guide them to take success to another level!

Bill Blankschaen, Writer, Author, Speaker, Founder of
StoryBuilders

RISE

Game-Changing
Success Strategies
for Women Leaders

JACKIE STALLINGS EVANS

Published by Sumter Press

Paperback 979-8-9899690-0-5

Hardback 979-8-9899690-1-2

eBook: 979-8-9899690-2-9

TABLE OF CONTENTS

DEDICATION

This book is dedicated to my heavenly family members: my mother, Mary Allen Stallings; my father, Reverend R.W. Stallings; and my brother, Dr. Ron J. Stallings. My parents gave me a solid foundation to deal with the mountains in my life. They taught me that there is always a way around the mountain, and to never let anyone close me into a box or steal my joy. My brother was my role model. He defied the odds as he became one of the first Black surgical oncologists in the world.

This book is also dedicated to my son, Michael Jamaal, who gave me my purpose.

And finally, to my heavenly pastor, Rev. Cameron M. Alexander, who delivered God's message each and every Sunday. God always sent him "just the right message" I needed to empower me to be resilient and stay the course.

Thanks to each of them for showing me that, "to whom much is given, much will be required" (Luke 12:48).

AUTHOR'S NOTE

Welcome to *Rise: Game-Changing Success Strategies for Women Leaders*! In the pages that follow, I share my personal experiences, insights, and hard-won wisdom gained from my time in various leadership roles at IBM. When I was hired, it was an exciting time to work for such a prestigious company. IBM computers helped to put the first man on the moon. My first project was Safeguard, an anti-ballistic missile project which alerted the President of the United States in the event that we were being attacked by Russia. Without a doubt, IBM was the leader in the technology industry, ranking in the top 10 on the Fortune 500 list of America's largest corporations. It was the preeminent technology company and a household name, much like Google, Apple and Meta are today.

Having started in an entry-level position a little more than a decade after the Civil Rights Act passed, and eventually retiring as an executive, I discovered the secret to success and how to effectively position myself for advancement. Upon leaving IBM, I transitioned to a full-time executive leadership coach.

Within the walls of IBM, I found myself perpetually standing out, not only as the sole person of color but also as the only woman in the room. In such a unique position, I faced the uphill challenge of charting my own course and discovering the strategies necessary to navigate within the organization successfully. Over the years, I have honed my expertise as a leadership coach, supporting clients who, like me, encounter numerous obstacles on their path to advancement.

This book serves as a culmination of my experience, knowledge, and the invaluable "lessons learned" I gained throughout my journey. The concepts covered in this book are from my perspective as a woman of color; however, these concepts include strategies and tools that apply to anyone aspiring to advance in their career as a leader. I present to you the Rising Leader model—a comprehensive five-part plan designed to empower women to bridge the gap between their current position and their future roles as leaders. It is the embodiment of my commitment to paying it forward, an opportunity to extend a helping hand to fellow businesswomen striving to achieve their leadership aspirations.

In the pages ahead, you will find a wealth of practical strategies, heartfelt anecdotes, and transformative insights. Together, we will explore the complexities of the corporate world, unpack the unique challenges faced by women in leadership, and uncover the keys to unlocking your full potential. This book is a guide, a mentor, and a source of inspiration as you embark on your own journey toward leadership excellence.

So, whether you are an ambitious professional seeking guidance, a woman of color facing the uphill battle of breaking through the glass ceiling, or someone dedicated to fostering diversity and inclusion in the workplace, this book is for you. I invite you to delve into its pages with an open mind and a readiness to embark on a transformational expedition. May it empower you, equip you, and embolden you to embrace your leadership journey with unwavering determination.

Here's What to Expect

This book is not meant to be a one-time read, but rather a valuable resource that you can return to time and time again. As you embark on this transformative journey, I encourage you to read it through from cover to cover, allowing the insights to sink in.

However, I also want to emphasize the importance of treating this book as a living, breathing companion on your path to leadership excellence. Highlight passages that resonate with you, jot down personal reflections and actionable steps in the margins, and create a roadmap for your own growth. Feel free to revisit specific chapters or sections that address your current challenges or areas of focus.

Let this book serve as your guidebook, ready to be consulted whenever you need a dose of inspiration, guidance, or a gentle reminder of the powerful principles that will propel you forward. This is your journey of growth and development, and I invite you to engage with the material actively, making it your own and integrating its wisdom into your leadership toolkit.

The following is an overview of how the book is arranged. This may be a handy index of sorts for you to revisit as you come back to the book again and again.

Part One: Overcoming the Barriers

In Part One, I lay the foundation for the journey ahead, equipping you with insights and strategies to navigate barriers. Through personal anecdotes, eye-opening statistics, and actionable steps, I invite you to challenge the status quo and forge your own path to leadership success.

Chapter One: You Don't Have to Move That Mountain

Chapter One draws from my personal experiences growing up during the Civil Rights Movement and my journey as a trailblazer in the corporate world. I begin by highlighting the persistent obstacles women of color encounter today. Despite progress, discrimination remains a significant issue. I share my own experiences and the statistics that reflect the ongoing struggles faced by these women. Inspired by my father's teachings, I share the concept of "Mountain Climbing Momentum" and offer practical tools to help you overcome barriers and navigate the corporate landscape.

Chapter Two: The Struggle is Real

Chapter Two delves deeper into the struggles and microaggressions faced by women of color in the workplace. I address the wage gap and the need for more advocates and sponsors to drive progress. Additionally, I explore the role companies can play in fostering an inclusive environment. This chapter empowers you to take control of your career, providing guidance on self-education and determination. You'll learn the importance of advocating for change within organizations and promoting diversity and advancement.

Part Two: The Rising Leader Model

In Part Two, we delve into the sections of the Rising Leader Model, guiding you through the essential aspects of personal development, relationship building, organizational understanding, community engagement, and self-care. Through practical tools, insights, and real-world examples, you'll be empowered to cultivate the skills and mindset necessary to thrive as a rising leader.

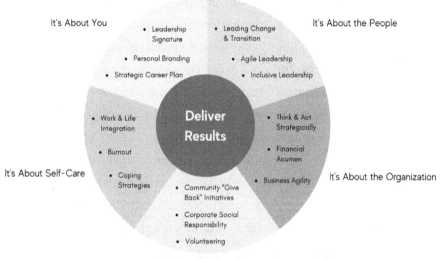

Rising Leader Model
Positioning Women Leaders to Advance in the Workplace

It's About You

- Leadership Signature
- Personal Branding
- Strategic Career Plan

It's About the People

- Leading Change & Transition
- Agile Leadership
- Inclusive Leadership

Deliver Results

- Work & Life Integration
- Burnout
- Coping Strategies

It's About Self-Care

- Think & Act Strategically
- Financial Acumen
- Business Agility

It's About the Organization

- Community "Give Back" Initiatives
- Corporate Social Responsibility
- Volunteering

It's About the Community

Section One: It's About You

Section One focuses on establishing a solid foundation by understanding, developing, and leveraging your unique Leadership Signature. We explore how your values, strengths, personality, and experiences contribute to your distinctive style of leadership. Discovering and communicating your Leadership Signature helps you differentiate yourself from others and position yourself as a compelling candidate for leadership roles.

I'll then guide you through crafting your personal brand statement by defining what you're known for and what you stand for, and delve into thinking more strategically about your career, overcoming career barriers, and presenting yourself effectively to others through Executive presence. You'll also craft a strategic career plan to position yourself to advance to the next level.

Section Two: It's About the People

Section Two emphasizes the shift in mindset required when transitioning into a new leadership role. It underscores the significance of building and nurturing relationships with your team, understanding their motivations, preferred recognition methods, skill sets, developmental needs, and personal goals. Effective delegation and fostering high-performing teams are essential leadership skills.

We explore the importance of leveraging diversity, encompassing not only gender and race but also cultural and generational differences. Additionally, we address the challenges of leading virtual teams in the modern workplace landscape.

Section Three: It's About the Organization

Section Three highlights the importance of being an agile and innovative strategic leader. I provide tools to develop your business acumen, which includes strategic, financial, and business agility. Understanding how your business operates, how it generates profits, and the key performance metrics helps to build credibility as a leader. By speaking the language of strategy and finance, and understanding the business, you enhance your ability to contribute to the organization's success and advance your career.

Section Four: It's About the Community

In Section Four, we explore the significance of community involvement for leadership growth. Engaging in volunteerism within your local community not only broadens your leadership skills, but also fosters positive public relations for your organization. We discuss the personal benefits of community engagement, including the opportunity to discover new interests, develop skills, gain confidence, and expand your network. Giving back to the community provides a sense of purpose and allows you to share your expertise, while also contributing to your growth as a leader.

Section Five: It's About Self-Care

Section Five discusses the importance of managing workplace stress and cultivating a support system, especially for a woman of color. No one reaches the top without help, a fact that emphasizes the need to prioritize self-care and build positive relationships with peers.

We look at the impact of workplace stress and burnout and discover self-care coping strategies. Additionally, we highlight how leaders can address burnout and foster a supportive culture. By implementing these practices, you can navigate challenges and thrive as a leader.

Your Leadership Success Journey

As you consume this content, you will gain a wealth of knowledge relative to ways to better equip yourself for the challenges of leadership roles and tackling gender bias and the barriers women face in the workplace.

Check in with your leadership team to gain their commitment to helping you advance. This is a partnership. You can only do your part. Your organization is also accountable for doing their part. This can include promoting your potential and performance when you're not in the room, nominating you for stretch assignments, publicly supporting you in leadership roles, and voicing support for your promotion.

I invite you now to embark on an empowering leadership success journey through the pages of this book. As you begin this journey, stay focused on the target in the center of the Rising Leaders Model. By consistently driving results and achieving milestones, you will undoubtedly make a lasting impact.

We are ready now to dive into Chapter One: "You Don't Have to Move That Mountain," where you will begin your journey to overcome barriers and unlock your leadership potential. Let's get started!

PART ONE
OVERCOMING THE BARRIERS

CHAPTER ONE

You Don't Have to Move That Mountain

*Obstacles are those frightful things
you see when you take your eyes off the goal.*
—Henry Ford

It had only been a few years since the Civil Rights Bill passed. My parents were active in the Civil Rights Movement and worked hard to desegregate the schools. They knew that separate was not equal and that every child, regardless of race, deserved a first-class education. You see, at Lincoln High, the local Black high school, we often got books passed down from Sumter High, the local White high school. Parents like mine wanted their kids to have freedom of choice. With the passage of the Civil Rights Bill, we felt that we had won the desegregation battle. We would soon learn that change was slow to come to Sumter.

It was a beautiful summer day in South Carolina, and it was my first day at the new school. I was a sophomore, one of a handful of Black students who transferred from Lincoln High to Sumter High.

During our summer break, my three best friends and I decided that we would transfer to Sumter High. I woke up that summer morning anxious about the new beginning. As my mom drove up to the school, protesters were outside with signs yelling racial slurs: "Go home n...." "We don't want you here." My mom was talking, but I didn't hear a word that she said as I was so focused on the protestors.

In that moment, my mind flashed back to the Little Rock Nine, a group of nine Black students who enrolled in Central High School in 1957, and little Ruby Bridges, who desegregated the all-White William Frantz Elementary School in New Orleans, Louisiana in 1960. I remembered how the federal marshals had to escort her to school every day for that entire year. I was feeling even more anxious as my mom and I walked through the doors of the school. What would the day be like?

As I walked down the hall to my first class of the day, a six-foot-tall blonde-hair blue-eyed guy stepped out in front of me. He towered over my five-foot-two frame and blocked my path. His buddies were right there with him like a pack of hyenas cheering him on. Without so much as a word, he looked right at me, hocked, and spit. It hit me right in the face.

My initial reaction was rage. I instinctively wanted to kick him as hard as I could, spit back at him, or fly at him with my fists. But, at that moment, I could see Dr. Martin Luther King saying this is a *non-violent* movement. I could hear my dad saying the way to win is not by violence, but by strategizing and out-thinking them.

So, I froze. I just stood there as the boys laughed and hurried down the hall. I silently walked on to class, seething within but stoic without.

I couldn't concentrate on any of my classes that day. All I could think about was how much I wanted revenge, yet I knew it was best not to retaliate. I didn't want my parents to be embarrassed if I got suspended from school because I had a moment of madness. When I went home that night, I didn't even tell them what had happened. I knew what they would say: *Handle it in a mature, non-violent way.* And I wasn't feeling that at all!

I thought it was best to take it to a higher authority. So, that night, as I routinely got on my knees to pray, instead of asking for advice, I asked God to burn the school down so I wouldn't have to go back the next day.

God said no.

Each day, I witnessed the cruelty of how we were treated at school. None of the teachers spoke up on our behalf. One night, as I kneeled down to pray, I asked God to show me a way to get around this huge mountain.

The next morning, before school started, I went into the principal's office. When I told him what had happened with the spitting incident, he lowered his chin, looked at me over the top rim of his glasses, and asked, "Well, what do you want me to do about it?"

Once again, my first reaction wasn't coming from my best self. I really wanted to snap right back at him: *You're the principal here, not me! What do* you *think you should do about it?* Instead, I politely informed him we had to do something, or someone was going to get killed—and their death would be on him.

If you consider that point in history and the location, it was a real possibility that this could happen. I couldn't even ride the school bus home because Black kids were beaten up every single day on the bus, including my boyfriend, who had no other options but the school bus.

I suggested that we form a committee of Black and White students to talk through the racial issues and recommend some things to do to resolve them. Of course, there were those White students who felt the only resolution was for us to go back to the Black school. And that wasn't about to happen. I'm not saying this committee really made much of a difference at the beginning, but I felt like it was at least a step in the right direction. The principal agreed.

My family used to love listening to the great Mahalia Jackson sing her famous gospel song, *Lord, Don't Move The Mountain*. It was an older song, but the lyrics were so appropriate to the Civil Rights struggles at the time:

> Oh Lord you don't have to move the mountain
> But give me the strength to climb
> And Lord, don't take away my stumbling blocks
> But lead me all around[1]

This song reminded me to be resilient and stay the course, not to let others steal my joy or change my path. So, I persisted, graduated, and went on to college. I decided to go to a Historical Black College and University (HBCU). I needed a safe and nurturing environment where I felt that I belonged. This was one of the best decisions ever. While at Hampton University, I pledged Alpha Kappa Alpha (AKA) sorority and realized the value of sisterhood. Even today, those same sisters are still in my life encouraging me along the way. It was here that I strengthened my shattered soul. During those years, I became confident in who I was and what I had to offer. Four years quickly passed, and I joined the working world.

A decade later, in 1988, on another beautiful fall day—this time in New York City—I stood in the boardroom of the IBM regional office. I was the Regional Sales Support Leader of a team that provided level-two technical support to our clients in the tri-state area (New York, New Jersey, and Connecticut). I was preparing to lead a kick-off meeting for a new initiative. As was usually the case, I was the only woman in the room and the only person of color.

As I was preparing my notes and PowerPoint, the Vice President of Sales, whom I had not yet met, came into the room and immediately walked up to me. I looked up and smiled. He introduced himself, then asked, "Would you mind getting me a cup of coffee?"

At that moment, 15-year-old Jackie from Sumter High School wanted to snap back, *Are your arms and legs broken? Get your own cup of coffee!* Luckily, once again, I was able to control that impulse. Instead, I politely replied, "Oh, you don't want me to make your coffee! I don't drink coffee and don't have a clue how to make it." Now, the coffee was right there in the room, so it would not have been difficult for him to walk over to the coffee pot and pour a cup.

Since this was the VP, and he would have to sign off on the new initiative I was introducing, I decided to not leave it there. I looked over and saw my colleague John—a caffeine junkie—and said, "John, please do me a favor and pour this gentleman one of your great cups of coffee."

When it came time to start the meeting, I stood up and began, "Good morning! Thank you all for coming; we're ready to begin! Today we're here to discuss a new initiative designed to minimize some of the issues we're having with supporting our product installations." I glanced over at the VP, whose eyes widened as he recognized his serious misassumption. At least he had the common decency to blush.

It's now more than four decades away from my being spit on in high school and three decades away from those boardroom assumptions, yet for Black women in America, has anything fundamentally changed?

Although sadly, it is still likely that as a woman of color someone could walk up to you and spit on you. And it is unfortunate but still probable that a Black woman might be assumed to be an assistant to a manager rather than the manager herself.

Prior to her newest engagement as Walgreens' CEO, Roz Brewer, who was CEO of Sam's Club at the time, was at a small roundtable event exclusively for chief executives in New York. During the reception, when introducing herself to a male CEO, he asked if she worked in marketing or merchandising. This was despite the fact that the invitation made it clear it was a CEO-only event.

"After I gave him the side-eye," Brewer says, "I ascended to the podium as the keynote for the day, and I enjoyed the look on his face when my bio was read. When you're a Black woman, you get mistaken a lot. You get mistaken as someone who could actually not have that top job."[2]

Statistics Tell the Stark Truth

Research on the state of women at work shows the same general pattern: "Women are having a worse experience than men. Women of color are having a worse experience than White women. And Black women, in particular, are having the worst experience of all."[3]

Black women are seriously underrepresented in management and executive roles despite the fact that they are more likely than all other groups of women and just as likely as all men to aspire to top executive roles.[4] Their motivation differs significantly, though. Black women are 50% more likely than men to say they are motivated by a desire to be role models for others like them. They recognize how difficult it can be for women of color to advance at work, and their goal is to change that.[5]

Despite their ambition, research also shows that Black women are more frustrated than White women about their path to the top. According to a report issued by the Center for Talent Innovation, 44% of Black women (compared to 30% of White women) reported feeling stalled in their careers. They were also more likely to feel that their talents weren't being recognized by their managers (26% versus 17%).[6]

It is clear that Black women are facing disproportionately high barriers in the workplace. They are affected by bias in hiring and promotions; Black women are promoted at a lower rate than White women at the first step up to manager, as is illustrated in the graphic below. Between the entry-level and the C-suite, the representation of women of color drops off by more than 75%. As a result, women of color account for only 5% of C-suite leaders, a number that hasn't moved significantly in the past four years.[7] Also noteworthy is that White men's representation increases in percentage at every leadership level, the only group to do so.

Representation in the Corporate Pipeline by Gender and Race
% of employees by level at the start of 2022

	Entry Level	Manager	Sr. Manager/ Director	VP	SVP	C-Suite
White Men	33%	41%	47%	54%	58%	61%
Men of Color	19%	19%	16%	14%	13%	13%
White Women	29%	27%	26%	24%	23%	21%
Women of Color	19%	14%	10%	8%	6%	5%

The Steep Climb

Mentorship and sponsorship are critical components required for advancing in your career, no matter your race. Statistically, less than a quarter of Black women feel they have the sponsorship they need to advance their careers. In one survey, 62% of women of color with some level of mentorship said the lack of an influential mentor was a barrier to their advancement.[8]

> Mentorship and sponsorship are critical
> components required for advancing in
> your career, no matter your race.

Melonie Parker, Chief Diversity Officer for Google, knows firsthand the difference mentorship can make. The following story recalls the time she was almost passed over for a promotion while working in the aerospace and defense industry years ago:

> At the time, she says, she was being tapped for a vice president role when a male mentor at the company, who was a senior-level VP, called her and told her, "Your manager is going to call you. He's going to try

to talk you out of [the job]. Don't let him talk you out of it. I will explain later."

Roughly thirty minutes after talking to her mentor, Parker says she received a call from her male manager saying, "Your name came up about this job, but you wouldn't like the location. I don't think you should do it."

"It played out just like my male mentor told me," Parker says. "And [my manager] was shocked when I said, 'Nope, I am interested. I do want to go through with the interview process."

Eventually, Parker landed the job. But, she says, it was only because she had a mentor at the company who gave her a heads-up about the bias that was at play. "I know I would have trusted my manager had I not gotten that phone call encouraging me differently," she explains. "I would've thought my direct manager had my best interest at heart."[9]

Nearly 75% of Black women view having a mentor as a key to success, but under 40% report having one. Of those that do have a mentor, about 30% have a Black male mentor, 30% have a White male mentor; 20% have another Black woman mentor, and less than 20% have a White female mentor.[10]

Before becoming an entrepreneur and CEO of my own company, What Do You Do When Leadership, Inc., I spent thirty years climbing the mountain of corporate leadership. That entire career was spent at IBM, a Fortune 100 company, with positions ranging from a programmer for an anti-ballistic missile project, to a technical sales representative, to a corporate facilitator/trainer, to a sales support leader, to a regional sales support leader, to new business opportunity manager, to IBM's Global Education & Training Executive, to a professional development leader, and ultimately retiring from the headquarters position as a Sales Learning Executive.

I was never assigned an official mentor or sponsor, so I had to seek and find guidance in other ways. Left on my own to figure out how to navigate within the company, I encountered more roadblocks than you can imagine. As I watched my peers move up in the organization, I realized getting to that executive level was a very steep climb for me. Somehow, that glass ceiling began to look like a cement ceiling.

Mentorship can come from different sources. Sometimes, you'll find a mentor in your own company, officially or unofficially. I had a couple of managers who I felt mentored me, even though it was never official. I also had women peers. We helped each other.

Other times, a mentor might be someone in your line of work but from outside of your company. It might even be just a trusted friend or family member, like my parents were to me.

Mountain Climbing Momentum

I spent years (many, many years!) as an *Only*—one of the only people of a certain race or gender at work. Women who are Onlys can have especially difficult day-to-day experiences. As the 2021 Women in the Workplace report describes it:

Onlys stand out, and because of that, they tend to be more heavily scrutinized. Their successes and failures are often put under a microscope, and they are more likely to encounter comments and behavior that leave them feeling othered, excluded, and reduced to negative stereotypes. Being an Only for one dimension of identity is already difficult. But women of color sometimes have to contend with being Onlys on two dimensions—both as the only woman in the room and as the only person of their race.[11]

Double Onlys tend to face even more bias, discrimination, and pressure to perform, and that was me—a woman *and* a person of color. My peers would often intimate that I was there because I was filling a quota.

One time, a male colleague referred to me as a double negative. My immediate response was to look at him in baffled amazement. I wanted to snap back at him and say, *Are you crazy?* I thought, *When God gave out brains, he definitely skipped over you.*

Instead, I composed myself and said, "Actually, I couldn't disagree with you more. In fact, I think of myself as a double positive. IBM gets to live up to their corporate commitment, and they get someone who delivers results to the business. Without a doubt, affirmative action opened the door for me to interview for the opportunity. But you'd better believe if I don't deliver, I won't be here."

Whether it was having my ideas at a brainstorming session virtually ignored or being told my management style was ineffective (it wasn't), if I had let these obstacles derail me from my purpose of continuing to succeed and grow in the business, it would have been a short-lived career.

Instead, I chose to see the obstacles differently. Every time something or someone stood in my way, I thought of my dad, a Southern Baptist preacher. Standing in the pulpit, wearing his big white robe, smiling out at the congregation, he would end his Sunday sermons with the following words:

> When you go down the road and you run into a
> mountain, I said… when you run into a mountain,
> if you can't go through the mountain, look to your
> right, look to your left, look over the mountain,
> look under the mountain—because there is always a
> way around the mountain.

I heard this message Sunday after Sunday, year after year while growing up. Between this and the Mahalia Jackson song I mentioned earlier, mountain metaphors were a big part of my childhood.

But it wasn't until I entered college, and then corporate America, that I began to truly understand. This was a message about adversity, perseverance, and staying the course. It was a story about the challenges that come in and out of our lives. Your mountain may be different from mine, but make no mistake about it, we all face obstacles in our lives. And there will be times when we have to be creative, pivot, and figure out a way to get around that mountain.

As a woman in Corporate America, there are full *ranges* of mountains. Just know there is a way around them. If you feel that you are stuck, not advancing, and need to figure out how to get around that mountain, this book is full of tools and strategies to help you.

If you are a woman in the workplace in America, and especially a Black woman, I have years' worth of wisdom to share that can help you bridge the gap between where you are now in your career and where you want to be.

In other words, as your virtual mentor in the pages that follow, someone who has walked the path ahead of you, my goal is to provide you with specific tools and strategies to make your way around the mountains you may face and into your next leadership position, whether you're in your first year of business, your fifth, or your fifteenth.

Former First Lady Michelle Obama said about former President Obama during her 2012 Democratic National Convention speech, "And he believes that when you've worked hard, and done well, and walked through that doorway of opportunity, you do not slam it shut behind you. You reach back and you give other folks the same chances that helped you succeed."[12]

I have been blessed to have had the opportunity to stand on the shoulders of giants, and now, for me, it is truly about giving back. Are you ready to learn strategies and tools to help you find your way around the mountain? If so, I'd be honored to be one of your mentors through this book.

Let's climb!

Key Takeaways

1. Black women are seriously underrepresented in management and executive roles despite the fact that they are more likely than all other groups of women and just as likely as all men to aspire to top executive roles.
2. Mentorship and sponsorship are critical components required for advancing in your career, no matter your race.
3. When there is a mountain in your way, there is a way around it.

CHAPTER TWO

The Struggle is Real

Obstacles don't have to stop you.
If you run into a wall, don't turn around and give up.
Figure out how to climb it, go through it, or work around it.
—Michael Jordan

Thinking outside of the box is a key value for IBM employees. In fact, the word THINK itself is trademarked by the company![1] The one-word slogan was introduced in 1911 by IBM founder Thomas J. Watson, Sr. During one of IBM's sales meetings, Watson interrupted, saying "The trouble with every one of us is that we don't think enough. We don't get paid for working with our feet—we get paid for working with our heads." Watson then wrote THINK on the easel. [2]

From that point on, the THINK sign appeared all over IBM offices, company publications, advertisements, and even in translated forms all over the world in IBM's offices. Whenever we had a meeting, people would say, "Let's brainstorm!" During our brainstorming sessions, the premise was that all ideas are good ideas and should be captured. Then, when we finished collecting ideas, we would circle back and discuss the pros and cons of each idea. Over time, brainstorming became the norm.

In one such session, the headquarters sales team was meeting to discuss some concerns that had been funneled up to the VP of Sales Support. The latest employee survey results indicated that our sales team felt they did not have the skills needed to perform at a high level. Upon digging deeper, we discovered that our sales team was not closing many deals where we clearly had a competitive advantage. The question was, why? Why weren't they closing the deals?

As usual, I was the only person of color in the room and one of just a few women. My manager, Scott, offered to facilitate the session. He jumped up to the whiteboard, marker in hand, and started jotting down the ideas being thrown out.

One idea was that we develop a training curriculum to address the problem. Scott jotted it down on the whiteboard. I suggested that we first needed to understand the reason our sales team was unable to close deals where we already had the advantage. What was getting in the way? Scott proceeded like he did not even hear me. Nothing went up on the whiteboard.

After a few minutes, I elaborated, "We have to understand what is getting in the way. What is the reason our sales leaders are not developing into high-performing sales reps? Once we understand that, then we can begin to facilitate some focus groups to really do a deep dive and uncover the issues that are getting in the way. Is this a global issue or just isolated to a particular sales region?" Scott paused, and when it was apparent that he was about to move on, I added, "Hey, Scott. Put it on the whiteboard."

Further into the session, I suggested that we get the local offices to identify their top performers and talk to them to understand what they were doing to achieve their results year after year. Once again, it didn't make it to the whiteboard.

Five minutes later, another colleague, Paul, said, "We've got to find out what's getting in the way of them being successful!" Well, up on the whiteboard that went, and then someone said, "Hey, Paul, I think you've got something there! I love that approach." Others chimed in with their agreement.

"Interesting..." remarked Scott. "Tell me more." I looked around the room trying to gauge if anyone else could see how this was *exactly the same idea* I had proffered minutes before, but everyone else just seemed focused on what my colleague was saying, nodding and murmuring in agreement. The next thing I knew, the idea—*my* idea, rephrased—was written on the whiteboard and tagged for further possible action. *I sat there steaming!*

I wish I could say I remember this incident because it was a one-time, memorable moment. But the truth is that this sort of dismissal happened more times than I could even begin to count. It happened so often, in fact, that it became the norm. And that was not okay with me.

I saw how they played the game. I was invisible to them. I just had to THINK of a better way to get my ideas respected. After all, I was the least of their concerns; their strategy was just to ignore me. But I was not going to walk away, say nothing, and let this continue to happen. As my dad would say, I just had to *find a way around the mountain.*

I had been here before. I learned early in life that I had to be smarter or better to stay in the game. I might get knocked down, but I learned from my failures how to bounce back and not get distracted from moving forward. I was more determined than ever to find my way around that mountain. (Battle on!)

Prior to the meeting, if I had to present, I would review my ideas with the influencers and decision-makers that would be in that meeting. I would say something like, "Hey, George, you know how we're meeting about *X* later this week? Well, I was thinking, what if we did blah blah blah?...What do you think?" My strategy was to approach them one-on-one, get their ideas, and, in some cases, incorporate both of our thoughts.

> I might get knocked down, but I learned from my failures how to bounce back and not get distracted from moving forward.

Sometimes I would get great ideas, and I would give them credit for it. I'd say, "What if we incorporate these ideas into the proposal; would you support this idea?" They'd say yes, and take pride in the fact that their ideas were incorporated.

By the time we got to the actual brainstorming meeting, I'd already made my rounds and had the key influencers familiar with my idea. That way, when I threw the idea out there, it was something they had already heard, had a part in the solution, and/or agreed it was a good idea. So up on the whiteboard it went! This turned out to be a winning strategy to help me get around the mountain.

In her book *Lead to Win: How to Be a Powerful, Impactful, Influential Leader in any Environment*, Carla A. Harris suggests another approach—one I wish I would have thought of thirty years ago! "When new ideas are introduced, if they are truly 'out of the box,' most participants in the discussion have a hard time grasping them. Typically, the idea needs to be introduced several times."

She goes on to say, "Selling your vision is one of the most important things you will do in your evolution from individual contributor to leader."[3]

Microaggressions

As women are promoted into leadership roles, their daily experiences often become more difficult. After leaving the entry-level position, these women are more than twice as likely to say they are Onlys (only woman) or Double Onlys (only woman *and* person of color). They are also more likely to have their competence challenged by being interrupted, receiving unsolicited comments on their emotional state, having their judgment questioned, or having their ideas ignored or dismissed. (Sound familiar?) Today such challenges are given a name: *microaggressions.*[4]

By almost any measure, Black women experience more microaggressions than other groups of women and are three to four times more likely than White women to be subjected to disrespectful comments and behavior.

Some of the microaggressions reported in the 2021 Women in the Workplace report include:

Microinsults:[5]

- Colleagues have touched my hair without my permission
- I have been told I'm "not like others" of my race/ethnicity
- I have repeatedly been told that I'm "articulate"
- Others have regularly taken credit for my ideas in meetings

- I have been excluded from meetings relevant to my job

- Others have mis-characterized me as "angry"

- I have been excluded or passed over for growth opportunities

- My manager has met one on one with others on my team, but not with me

Microinvalidations:[6]

- Colleagues have asserted that they are "color-blind" (e.g. "I don't see race.")

- I have to explain what it's like to live as a person of my race/ethnicity

- I have been mistaken for someone else of the same racial background

- Colleagues have told me they have friends of my race/ethnicity

- Colleagues have asserted they're not racist

Microassaults:[7]

- Colleagues have used racially insensitive language around me

I've had experience with a variety of microaggressions, and I'm sure my experiences are similar to those of many women and people of color. One of the most common I have personally heard over the years comes from people who have not met me in person but with whom I've spoken on the telephone (in the age before Zoom!). If I made a comment about my culture, their response would always be, "Oh! You're so articulate. You don't sound Black!" I always want to say back to them, "Oh really? And what does Black sound like?" But, as our former First Lady,

Michelle Obama, so eloquently said, "When they go low, we go high."

I wish that I could say this is rare; however, according to one report, 26% of Black women said they have heard others express surprise at their language skills or other abilities, whereas only 14% of all women say the same.[8]

A colleague of mine, also Black, was on a phone call with a man who even made a blatantly racist comment, expecting her to laugh along in agreement. When she called him out on it, his sputtered apology about "not meaning anything by it" and "didn't mean to offend you" fell flat. They both knew that he didn't realize she was Black.

Another woman I worked with had an African name, not easy to pronounce. Her boss was a man who not only couldn't pronounce her name, but didn't even try to do so. Instead, he gave her a nickname, and despite her constant correction of, "That's not my name!" he persisted. She finally left her job.

Alejandra, a Latina woman, shared, "When I started grad school, the intro class was taught by two White women, and I was one of two Mexican-Americans in the cohort. They constantly called me Maria, the other girl's name... we look nothing alike."

Kieran was going to a company lecture on math."I walked over a few minutes early, and in the room, two men were already seated. One of the men saw me and quickly asked if I was looking for a talk on design that was being held nearby. He assumed that, as a woman, I would not be interested or able to go to a math talk."

The Wage Gap

In addition to having to deal with microaggressions, women of color have to deal with equal work and performance not being rewarded with equal pay. The disparity in wages between men and women continues to widen. This has been a focal point of discussion for years, from Hollywood to Corporate America and everywhere in between.

According to a Pew Research analysis of median hourly earnings of both full- and part-time workers, the gap in pay between men and women has remained about the same over the past twenty years. Women tend to earn roughly 82% of what men earn. "It would take an extra 42 days of work for women to earn what men did in 2020 (for the same job)." [9]

Women of color know that those statistics don't tell the whole story, because non-White workers, male or female, earn less than White men (with the exception of Asian men, who earn slightly more).

In a study of U.S. workers with a four-year college degree, it was found that Black and Hispanic women come in at only about 70% of the hourly wages of White men,[10] and some broader studies (including non-degreed workers) show the percentage to be even lower than that. At the current trajectory of pay increases, it would take Black women until the year 2130 to reach equal pay.[11]

"If the gender pay gap were eliminated, on average, a Black woman working full-time year-round would have enough money for more than two-and-a-half years of childcare, more than two-and-a-half additional years of tuition and fees for a four-year public university, or 22 more months of rent, according to the National Partnership for Women & Families."[12]

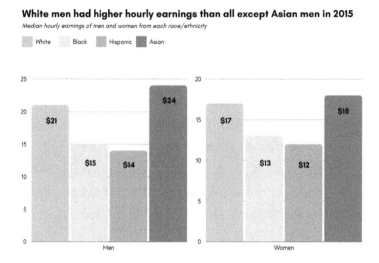

White men had higher hourly earnings than all except Asian men in 2015

Median hourly earnings of men and women from each race/ethnicity

White   Black   Hispanic   Asian

For a short time, I shared an office with Linda, another manager at IBM who also happened to be a Black woman. We did the same job but were responsible for different parts of the business. One particular day, she went into the copier room to pick up a document she sent to the printer there. As she picked up the stack of papers, she realized that her manager had also printed something just before her: salary information for her group.

Of course, she couldn't help but see it, and when she realized what she was looking at, she had already registered that she was being paid $65,000 annually while all the White men in the group were making $100,000 for doing the *same job*. What was so apparent to Linda was that she was performing at a higher level than the men who were making that higher salary.

She was in the awkward position of not being able to say anything about it to her manager because technically she wasn't supposed to have seen it. Since she was leaving in a matter of days for her maternity leave, she kept it to herself.

Before she returned to work, her manager actually contacted her at home and told her she was going to be getting a salary increase. She said, "Really? I just got an increase three months ago!" Linda's manager said that she had asked Human Resources to compare the salaries of people in her group, and the comparison revealed that she should have a pay increase.

The good thing is that when the manager discovered the discrepancy, she did something about it. We need more leaders and advocates to speak up and make the needed changes to get rid of wage disparities.

In another example, a coaching client of mine, Renee, was a director for a manufacturing company. Under her direction, her team exceeded revenue and profit year after year. Because they were a private company, they did whatever they wanted to do in terms of compensation for employees. The good ol' boy network was alive and well.

> We need more leaders and advocates to
> speak up and make the needed changes
> to get rid of wage disparities.

There were a number of red flags Renee observed before she picked up the phone and called me to ask for my help.

The first red flag occurred during a conversation Renee had with one of her peer managers, Mona. Like Renee, Mona was at a director level. Mona told Renee that she was promoting Ted, a White man on her team who was a level lower. When Renee asked what the salary range was for Ted's current lower level, she found out that he was already earning $60K more annually than she was, despite her higher level.

The second red flag occurred when Renee changed managers. The first thing her new manager told her was that he needed to bring her salary up because there were people in the same department at a lower level with less responsibility making much more than she was. Her manager told her that since it was such a sizable increase, he could not do it all at once. He would have to give her bigger increases over several years. This is exactly what leaders should do: correct wage discrepancies when they see them.

The final red flag occurred when Renee had a Black male employee reporting directly to her. He informed Renee that he knew he was underpaid and was leaving the company. As Renee began to look for a replacement, HR presented her with two candidates. The first candidate was being offered $115K. This was $35K more than Renee's direct report was being paid. In fact, the new hire would also be earning more than Renee!

The next recruit HR presented her with was being considered for a job two levels below Renee; HR proposed offering this candidate $200K. Renee began to think about leaving the company, but before doing so, she decided to talk to HR. She discussed the fact that her job responsibilities did not align with her salary. In many cases, she was being paid less than her direct reports that were two levels below her. HR told her that there were two reasons this was the case: One, she went to an HBCU (historically Black college/university), and two, it was this manufacturing company that made her who she was.

Renee challenged HR on both of those comments. HR was definitely on a slippery slope, as both responses were insensitive and downright stupid responses to give to an employee. At that point, Renee called me. She discussed the situation and asked for my help. As her executive coach, I advised her to gather as much data as possible to support her case. She pulled her job description, went through it, highlighted everything she was doing, highlighted the results achieved, and highlighted the value she was bringing to the company.

Renee then went online and researched salary comps and salary ranges for her job based on demographics. Armed with that data, she was prepared to meet with her VP of Manufacturing. Shortly after her discussion, she called to tell me that she was getting a $45,000 increase.

As a further result, her company hired an HR compensation specialist to ensure equity among the salary ranges of all employees.

The Need for More Advocates

On May 25, 2020, the world witnessed another pandemic—the pandemic of systemic racism and racial injustice—as the world watched the senseless death of George Floyd, a 46-year-old Black man who was murdered in Minneapolis, Minnesota. For many, this was the first time they were confronted face-to-face with racial injustice. It left many of us saying, "It could have been my son."

After the death of George Floyd, many of my White coaching colleagues flooded social media expressing their concern and acknowledging that they never realized that this type of systemic racism was taking place. These colleagues began to host panel discussions, creating a safe environment where our White colleagues felt comfortable asking questions without fear of saying the wrong thing or offending in order to better understand the challenges that people of color face in the workplace.

As one of the panelists, it was truly a humbling experience to share and have my White colleagues feel safe enough to ask those tough questions that enabled them to better understand what people of color experience on a day-to-day basis. Having these types of conversations is key to understanding, and only then can change begin.

For the first time in my life, corporations were speaking up, acknowledging, and proclaiming their position relative to racial injustice. The world was starting to see something that it had never seen before. All races started coming together to demand fair treatment. The momentum toward change continues to build, and it is up to us as leaders to sustain it.

Now that corporations have spoken up against racial injustice, it is time to follow through and implement plans to change things. So many people are saying, *But I do not know what to do within the corporation.*

Let me just stop and say this: I am not a diversity, equity, and inclusion (DE&I) specialist, nor have I ever worked in Human Resources (HR). These are the experts. My comments are based solely on what I have experienced as a Black woman working in Corporate America in a leadership role. I worked in the trenches and was responsible for making a profit for my organization.

> Now that corporations have spoken up against racial injustice, it is time to follow through and implement plans to change things.

I have intentionally titled this section "The Need for More Advocates" versus "The Need for More Allies." Like a workplace ally, a workplace advocate often utilizes a position of privilege, but rather than just providing support to an underrepresented group, an advocate will defend, write, or speak on their behalf to ensure fair and accurate representation.

While 67% of White employees say they are allies to their colleagues who are women of color, statistics show that *less than half* of them actually take action to call out bias or advocate for advancement or new opportunities for these women.[13] And oftentimes the actions White employees prioritize are not the actions the women of color find most meaningful.

As a result of the continuing challenges Black women deal with each day in the workplace, they tend to see their company's commitment to their advancement as lacking—lots of talk, little effective action.

There is much work to be done! Here are some things to consider: [14]

What Companies Can Do

Overall, leaders must be made accountable. We must put policies and procedures in place to measure progress. Here is a short but not inclusive list of things that can be done to drive change:

- *Ask women what they are experiencing and what they need:* Gathering data on the experiences women are having in the workplace will help you develop a better plan of action. There are multiple ways to do this, e.g., pulse surveys, interviews, focus groups, social media, or check-ins.

- *Benefits:* Develop and communicate across the organization the business benefits of an inclusive organization and how it has helped the company. Research has shown many benefits in the workplace: higher revenue growth, greater readiness to innovate, and increased ability to recruit a diverse talent pool.

- *Assess your current workforce*: Make women of color advancement a business priority by setting targets and metrics that take into account both gender and race.

- *Hold leaders accountable*: Put these metrics into leaders' yearly performance objectives. Measure metrics, share metrics, and reward progress.

- *Recruit/Hire:* Establish clear, specific, and consistent hiring criteria to minimize decisions based on subjectivity. Consider making the resumes and assignments anonymous for all candidates. Remove any names, colleges or organizations which may identify the candidate as a person of color.

- *Wages:* Conduct an assessment to ensure that employees are being paid for performance vs. based on the "good ol' boy network." Ensure that salaries are equitable. Stop making excuses about the guidelines; we all know guidelines can be changed.

- *Culture:* Create a more inclusive culture by developing specific conduct guidelines. Implement a process to respond to and resolve discrimination. Conduct yearly diversity, equity, and inclusion meetings to encourage colleagues to share their experiences in the workplace and help them to take on the lens of another person's experience. Provide training to help employees understand the effects of gender stereotyping. Develop a formal process to anonymously report biased situations in the workplace and share results so employees understand this will not be tolerated in the workplace.

* *Pipeline:* Evaluate promotions and talent development to ensure quality professionals are in the pipeline. Provide honest *feedback* that is real-time. I scheduled checkpoint meetings for all employees to share their personal growth and developmental areas. Be specific. You cannot improve if you do not know what you need to do. This can be difficult when there is an element of race, gender, or age. I conducted quarterly reviews for all employees and clarified what they were doing well and what they needed to improve on. Having those tough conversations during the year is not nearly as tough as waiting to have those tough conversations during year-end performance evaluations. No surprises…when they walked in the door for their year-end review, they already knew their year-end performance rating. So, during the session, we focused on lessons learned and what they would like to accomplish in the next year. All employees deserve this. Only when you are honest and upfront will you earn their trust.

* *Male Advocates:* Women need more male advocates in the workplace. It is a win-win situation for both women and men. Male advocacy is important for two reasons. First, increasing diverse participation is not just a woman's issue. Diversity and inclusivity are business issues. There

are so many facts that show how diverse perspectives bring more company innovation and competitiveness to the table. Second, depending on the industry, men may hold a majority of formal and informal positions of power within the organization. This is true in the tech industry. They have a great deal of influence and are often in a position to influence these dynamics compared to most women.[15]

I spoke to a couple of men who told me that they want to advocate for women, but they just do not know how. Some of these things that men can advocate for include:

- Advocating to change the environment to a more inclusive environment.

- Advocating for individual and systemic change. Call out inequities—the seen and unseen. If you know a woman deserves a promotion, speak up. Talk to the manager who has the power to promote her. Or, if you notice in a meeting that a woman's voice is not being heard, speak up, be diplomatic, and make a comment for her to be heard.

- Give credit where credit is due.

- Listening is one of the most important ways for a male to be an advocate. Educate yourself by listening to the experiences of women counterparts, understanding their issues, and figuring out how to go about addressing them.

- Speak up when you hear sexist or racist language.

- Be a mentor and sounding board.

It is a win-win situation for both women, men, and the organization.

- *Sponsors/Mentors:* Develop a process to help them navigate through the organization. Be intentional about matching mentors and sponsors to qualified women of color in an effort to grow the executive pipeline, to help them be recognized for their accomplishments and possible promotion.

- *Benchmark:* Benchmark and learn from other companies that are making progress in diversity, equality, and inclusion.

Just Show Them

It would have been easy for me to just give up hope of advancing my career given the numerous roadblocks I encountered simply because of my race and gender. In fact, at one point early on in my career, I was heading down a slippery slope that might have taken me in that direction.

I was going through a nine-month new-hire training program along with about forty other new employees. Of that group, only 9% were women of color. We were in the first six-week segment of the program when one evening Al, Debbie, and I met up to work on our homework assignment.

Right away, Debbie and I started complaining about how unfairly we were being treated because we were Black, how much harder we had to work, and so on. Al spoke up saying, "You know, you can spend all of your time complaining, or you can show them they are wrong. Stop creating all of that negative energy, and just show them." That advice has stayed with me throughout my life's journey. Thank you, Al.

Debbie and I looked at each other like, "He's right." From that point on, we moved forward to "show them." We finished the program, and in fact, Al was voted most likely to become CEO of IBM. There was no doubt in any of our minds that he could be IBM's CEO. Perhaps he was ahead of his time in terms of IBM having a Black CEO. Al went on to move up within IBM quickly leading various general management roles. His love was running Software businesses. In September 2021, he was elected to the IBM Board of Directors.

The current generation of millennials is showing a significant shift in attitude from accepting that "this is just how things are" to "Enough is enough!" When you make that decision to take your career into your own hands, educate yourself on how to advance professionally, and determine to "show them" nothing is going to stand in your way, you may just find that the concrete ceiling is ready to crack and crumble.

> When you make that decision to take your career into your own hands, educate yourself on how to advance professionally, and determine to "show them" nothing is going to stand in your way, you may just find that the concrete ceiling is ready to crack and crumble.

In the coming chapters, I will walk you through The Rising Leader Model. Get ready to dive deep and discover what you need to know in order to successfully lead yourself, your team, your organization, your community, and to focus on your self-care.

Key Takeaways

1. Women are more likely to have their competence challenged through microaggressions—by being interrupted, receiving unsolicited comments on their emotional state, having their judgment questioned, or having their ideas ignored or dismissed.

2. Women of color have to deal with equal work and performance not being rewarded with equal pay.

3. Companies play a major role in helping to close these gaps. They must put policies and procedures in place to measure progress and hold leaders accountable.

4. Women need more male advocates, sponsors, and mentors in the workplace. They make a difference.

5. When you make that decision to take your career into your own hands, educate yourself on how to advance professionally, and determine to "show them" that nothing is going to stand in your way, you may just find that the concrete ceiling is ready to crack and crumble.

PART TWO
RISING LEADER MODEL

SECTION ONE
IT'S ABOUT YOU

If you can't figure out your purpose, figure out your passion.
Your passion will lead you right into your purpose.
—T.D. Jakes

After graduating from Hampton University with a degree in math, I was energetic and ready to show IBM how *brilliant* I was by helping them solve problems. I was eager to show the world that people of color should not be judged by the color of their skin but rather by the content of their character. I would show them. I had it *all* figured out. But little did I know that college textbook learning was not the "real world."

What I didn't know then, but quickly learned, was that I could know everything there was to know about the "technical" side of IBM's products, but it wouldn't advance me to a leadership role until I understood the strategic and financial side of the business—profit/loss, metrics, strategic planning, product development, and so forth. That's when I decided to go back to graduate school for my MBA.

Stand in Your Authenticity

As you advance within the organization, you will be faced with tough decisions. Knowing who you are, what you value, and what you stand for makes those tough decisions easier to make. Defining what makes you unique forms the foundation of how you lead your life. It is what defines your authentic self.

Rashida Jones, President of MSNBC and the first Black woman to run a major news network encouraged 2020-2021 graduates of Hampton University to stand in their authenticity: "...Discover what gets you inspired, or outraged, or whatever it is inside of you that drives you forward. Because whatever you're going to do with the next five, ten, or even forty years of your life, it's got to be something you believe in and you're passionate about."[1]

When a person is authentic, they are able to speak their opinions honestly in a healthy way, pursue their passion, listen to their inner voice to guide them forward, and make decisions that align with their values and beliefs. But, most importantly, when you live your authentic life, you allow yourself to be vulnerable and open-hearted.

This is really hard to do when you do not have that foundation defined or when you are not comfortable with who you are. We all have gone through some "stuff" in our lives, but when you use that as a learning curve, it helps you to be confident and stand firmly in your authenticity.

At this stage of my life, I did not know what I was passionate about. My dad told me he always knew he wanted to be a minister because of his love for God. My mother knew she wanted to be a teacher. And, at the age of 14, my brother knew he wanted to be a pharmacist. He would always tell me, "Jackie, just imagine it, *Stallings and Stallings Pharmaceuticals*." He went on to become one of the first Black students to graduate from the University of South Carolina in the School of Pharmacy. He always said, "I graduated #2 and should have been #1, but they weren't about to let a Black person graduate #1." He went on to become one of the first Black surgical oncologists in the world.

Growing up in Sumter, the role models I saw were ministers, teachers, doctors and lawyers. I always said, "I don't know what I want to be when I grow up." That is why it is so important to see role models that look like you and me. It plants the seed inside of you knowing that anything is possible.

After graduating from college, I joined the IBM Corporation. It seemed like the best decision for me. I had always been taught "knowledge is power," and IBM's training program far exceeded that of other companies.

I was always clear about the things I was passionate about, but it was not until years later in life that my passion led me to my purpose. My purpose is to give back to others what I have been so blessed to have learned and experienced in life.

While at IBM, our VP of Sales Learning, Milt, felt that executive coaching was one way to develop our sales leaders, so everyone on his leadership team became certified coaches. I could see how coaching made a difference in the sales leaders' performance. Being able to introduce them to leadership strategies and concepts that helped to make them more effective leaders was something I loved to do.

After leaving IBM, I started my coaching/consulting practice and continued to coach. So many of my clients would tell me, "Nobody has ever told me that." I shared with my girlfriend,

Linda, that I was surprised so many of my clients did not know these basic strategies. I'll never forget what she told me.

She had worked for IBM, Sprint, and AT&T. She said, "Jackie, all training programs are not the same. None of those companies that I worked for trained their people like IBM. What may be basic to you is not to everyone."

It was at that moment that I realized my purpose—to share what I learned during my leadership journey, sharing my gifts, and helping clients advance to the next level.

One important thing is to know what makes you unique. It is this foundation that will help you navigate through the storms in your life. That foundation of knowing who you are and the value you bring to the table is your competitive advantage. That foundation is built by understanding, developing, and capitalizing on your unique leadership signature. Your leadership signature is like your personal name signature or your thumbprint. It is your uniqueness. It is what you bring to the table that differentiates you.

There is no one way to lead. There is no one leadership style that is more effective than all the other leadership styles. A leader is effective when they develop their own unique way of leading. By defining my leadership signature, I was able to find my inner power, be confident standing in my power, and be comfortable expressing my authentic voice.

CHAPTER THREE

Leadership Signature

In the future, there will be no female leaders.
There will just be leaders.
—Sheryl Sandberg

Your leadership signature is based on who you are, your values, strengths, improvement areas, personality, and experiences. It's your own unique style of leading. It is made up of three primary components—your uniqueness, your credibility, and your self-efficacy.

Your Uniqueness

What are your unique values and beliefs that lead your life? What things are core to who you are? I often take my clients back to their childhood experiences to uncover their values and core beliefs. What were the core values in your family? Which of your core values will guide your behavior as you step into a leadership role? What were the things that were drilled into you from a very young age and programmed into your brain?

For me, being trustworthy and honest were key values and beliefs that have always guided my decisions and actions. What about you? What are the core values and beliefs that guide you? What motivates and influences your vision and decision-making?

Your Credibility

Knowing who you are and feeling comfortable in your own skin is the foundation for becoming an effective leader. What gives you credibility with others? What is it about you that others want to follow? Credibility is a key leadership capability, but not everyone has that. When you are credible, you practice what you preach. You are respected because you keep your commitments and lead with a strong sense of purpose.

Your Self-Efficacy

Women in business are often told they need to have confidence to succeed. *Believe in yourself*, it's said, *and you can do anything!*

But is it really confidence? Based on my experience as a coach and a leader, I want to offer this distinction between confidence and self-efficacy.

Confidence can be defined as a feeling or belief in oneself, one's abilities, and one's judgments. It is a state of mind that arises from a sense of competence, self-assuredness, and positive self-esteem.

I believe that self-efficacy is a more accurate description of what we need as leaders. Self-efficacy is about having a strong positive belief that you can figure it out, and that you have the capacity and the skills to achieve your goals. It is the self-belief that a person can perform a difficult task or cope with adversity.

The process of developing self-efficacy is not always easy. It requires a high level of self-awareness and recognition of our innate strengths, our past experiences, knowing when to ask for help, who to turn to, and how to negotiate for what is needed. It keeps one optimistic that they can achieve the desired outcome.

Self-efficacy can facilitate setting goals, being persistent in the face of barriers, and one's ability to recover from setbacks. It is your *resilience factor*.[2]

This belief that a person can perform a difficult task or cope with adversity is a skill that can be fostered and strengthened. I often ask my clients to think about times when they stepped into a leadership role. What was it that gave them the belief that they could do it? Their responses fell into one of four areas:

+ It was their expertise in that area, such as finance, technology, or marketing, which gave them a higher level of self-efficacy.

+ It was because they had done it before and felt they could do it again.

+ It was their people or their emotional intelligence skills that enabled them to position the situation where others would follow.

+ And for some, it was their love for a challenge and being energized by taking a risk, jumping into the current crisis, and solving it.

This exercise of recalling past experiences helped them to understand what drives their self-efficacy and often helped them move from being stuck to action. So, what is it for you? What drives and motivates you to take that next step?

Research tells us that young men and women enter the workforce with similar levels of confidence, but within two years, women's confidence plummets while men's confidence continues to rise over their careers. Women's confidence begins to rise a little later in their careers, after the initial decrease.[3]

I experienced this firsthand when I joined IBM full of confidence, but like so many other women, soon experienced that nagging inner voice. *Do I trust myself? Should I speak up? What will other people say about me? Do I need to be careful not to outshine others? I'm not good at this.*

So, what happens? What causes a woman's confidence to plummet? As I have reflected more deeply, I've found that it stems from one or more of the following four issues: a communication issue, a competency issue, a cultural issue, or a lack of feedback. By addressing these causes, we continue to build and strengthen the self-efficacy muscle.

Communication Issue

Have you offered your ideas in a meeting, and they were ignored? Did you know what you were trying to say but weren't confident in the way you communicated it? Or maybe what you communicated wasn't well received?

To improve communication, some practices you can implement include:

- Asking questions to clarify
- Showing interest in what others say and do
- Using humor to make your important points and to lighten the discussion
- Expressing your ideas respectfully versus being confrontational

○ If someone's idea differs from yours, you might say, "Help me understand your reason for thinking this way," or "I see this a little differently."

- Clarifying your idea
  ○ Maybe it was ignored because it was not understood. Or maybe it was ignored because of the other person's ego. Which is it? Try to figure out what makes them tick and put a plan in place to get your idea heard.

It may just be that you need to improve your verbal communication skills. Perhaps you could benefit from a refresher course in public speaking or join a Toastmasters Club where speaking and leadership skills are learned and practiced in a welcoming and encouraging environment. There are a number of tools that will help in this area.

Competence Issue

Oftentimes, moving into a new position, a new company, or an entirely new career can leave you feeling as though your skills for the job may not be up to par. If you struggle with feeling competent, think about it in terms of skill set.

Ask yourself:

- What skills do I need to be effective in this job?

- What skills am I less confident about? How can I develop those skills?

- What skills am I confident in using? How can I leverage those strengths to gain more visibility in my role?

- How can I change my behavior to demonstrate my confidence to others?

Culture Issue

Research shows that when women are in male-dominated environments, they feel less confident and are less willing to speak up and share their ideas. It's often difficult to be viewed as one of the insiders when it comes to the "good ol' boy" network; however, skills such as networking, negotiating, and influencing others are vital for progression to senior roles. Women must be courageous and step outside of their comfort zone into an environment where they feel the culture rarely supports them.

One of my clients, Mona, organized a regional meeting. The men decided to plan a separate golf afternoon, and she was not invited. When Mona found out, she was steaming, but thought it was best to remain silent.

> Skills such as networking, negotiating, and influencing others are vital for progression to senior roles.

The next week during our coaching session, she brought this up as a topic. After our coaching session, she decided that when she had the opportunity, she would speak up and let them know that she loves to play golf and would love to go with them the next time. Mona told me that stepping outside of her comfort zone and using her voice to address the issue was a freeing feeling for her.

Feedback Issue

The lack of feedback, or mixed feedback, can bring a woman's confidence level down. When it comes to performance, women are not getting the feedback they need to help them advance to the next level. Asking for specific feedback more directly is one way that can help to advance your career and help you to continue to build your self-efficacy.

Giving and receiving feedback is important. It helps you to figure out what's working and what you can do differently. Feedback also lets you know how others perceive you. Perception is real. You may not agree with the feedback, but it helps to know how you are being perceived. And, if that is not the way you want to be perceived, feedback gives you an opportunity to change.

Other Strategies to Help Increase Self-Efficacy

Women often have self-limiting beliefs that prevent them from stepping out of their comfort zone. Recognizing and challenging self-limiting beliefs helps to increase self-awareness and self-efficacy and can help us shift these beliefs over time.

Start by identifying and challenging your self-limiting beliefs. What thoughts are holding you back and preventing you from taking action? Challenge them by searching for evidence to disprove them. For example, if you are an introvert and, as a result, are quiet in meetings, challenge yourself to participate more often.

Utilize positive visualization. Another strategy to help you increase your self-efficacy and improve your performance is positive visualization. When we visualize an act, the brain generates an impulse that tells us that we can perform it. This motivates us to pursue that goal.

When you have a well-defined idea of what you want to achieve, you are able to identify the steps to make it a reality. One of my clients, Usha, said that she stands in front of the mirror and says, "I love me. I am worth it." Telling herself these empowering words helped motivate her to move forward.

Change your mindset. Being self-aware helps you become aware of how you're thinking and how you're talking to yourself. Be cognizant and think about your mindset. It's like turning the volume down on that little voice inside your head or changing the channel.

Focus on the strengths you possess and your achievements. Avoid negative self-talk. Be optimistic, because your outward behavior will portray your inner feelings. The mindset theory that was developed by Stanford University researcher Carol Dweck shows that the key to success is not ability, but whether an individual believes their abilities are a fixed mindset or a growth mindset.

Fixed mindset individuals avoid situations that might expose their limitations, preventing them from stepping outside their comfort zone and taking risks. However, a growth mindset individual sees everything as a learning opportunity that can move them closer towards the achievement of their goals.

Celebrate your accomplishments. So often we do a good job but never stop to acknowledge it. Pat yourself on the back. Be your own cheerleader. It is food for the soul to pause and say, "I did it! Good job!"

For me, this prepares me for the next challenge because I now know, having accomplished the previous goal despite its challenges, I can accomplish the next task by being persistent and resilient.

> It is food for the soul to pause and
> say, "I did it! Good job!"

Implement power practices. I learned this from my son, Michael. He played basketball, and before each game, he would listen to his favorite song to pump him up. Some people wear their favorite clothes or favorite colors. When I want to feel confident, I put on my "power red." I've seen some of my clients do a certain body stance, for example, standing tall. You can also talk to a supportive friend or even your coach to help you feel strong and confident.

Practice. To venture out of your comfort zone is difficult and scary. But I tell my clients to take small steps and make small successes. These small successes will boost your resilience.

The overall manner in which you behave will transmit a feeling of confidence to others. For example, President Obama walked with a swift, confident stride.

Speak up in meetings and interact with people in large gatherings versus talking with two or three people in a small group the entire evening. Watch your speech because what you say and how you say it transmits a great deal about how people perceive you. Vary your pitch and the tone of your voice. Pause for emphasis and avoid using words such as "er" and "umm" and filler phrases like "you know."

Being mindful of incorporating these strategies will help you build your self-efficacy.

Assess Your Leadership Signature

Your Leadership Signature is a lifelong journey of self-development and leadership development. It can often feel like two steps forward and one step back. It takes courage and commitment to be on this journey. It is an awesome and rewarding journey. It changes not only your life but the lives of those you lead! I applaud you for stepping forward to lead.

Now that you have defined your leadership signature, your unique way of leading, it is time to step into your power.

CHAPTER FOUR

Step into Your Power

*There is no force more powerful
than a woman determined to rise.*
—W.E.B. Du Bois

As the world becomes more competitive, companies and leaders have to be able to build trust among their current and prospective clients. And as social media becomes one of the primary vehicles for being known, it is even more important for a leader to showcase their leadership skills. One way of doing this is by developing and establishing a personal leadership brand.

Personal branding on social media allows a leader to share their expertise with others. It also benefits the company by attracting clients, partners, and talent. Using social media as a platform to showcase their brand can lead to attracting and building a bigger audience that cares about their industry.

The personal leadership brand is a snapshot of who you are as a leader, what you value, and what differentiates you from others. It sums up what you stand for and how you do it. There are several benefits to having a leadership brand.

- It communicates your reputation and the value that you offer to an employer. And it is a great way to highlight your expertise within the organization.

- It highlights your values, strengths, goals, and performance history.

- It often defines what makes you successful as a leader.

- When you are clear on what you want to be known for, it allows you to focus and let go of those activities that do not let you deliver on your brand. It guides your thinking, decisions, actions, and your behavior as a leader. It can enhance your ability to achieve your professional and career goals.

- It can help you build trust and credibility.

- When your brand is known, you control how people speak about you when you are not present.

- It can help you broaden and deepen your impact within your community.

- It can often lead to being established and recognized in your industry as a thought leader. This opens up opportunities for you within and outside of the organization. Some of my clients have been asked to participate in panel discussions on their topic and to partner with like-minded leaders and/or companies within and outside of their organizations.

- It is an opportunity to get feedback from others as to how they perceive you. And if that is not the way you want to be perceived, you can change that perception.

What is your Purpose?

A personal brand statement should be created with a purpose in mind. This is an important place to start because the brand statement is designed to help you achieve your purpose.

My client Jean wanted to be promoted and needed to change the perception that she was difficult to work with. Ariana wanted to increase her company's confidence in her as a leader. And Jacqui wanted to clarify her talents to make it easier for her to land opportunities.

Craft Your Personal Leadership Brand

Your personal leadership brand is based on your beliefs, life experiences, work experiences, personality, and your desire to have an impact on your business, stakeholders, and society at large. It is designed the same way that one develops a brand statement for a product, service, or company.[4]

Step 1: What are the results that you want to achieve and by when?

Start with the end in mind. Identify your audience and focus on their needs. Who are the people that you need to sell your brand to? What are their pain points? What is the problem that you can help them solve? There are basically four groups to examine:

- **Customers:** What do your customers want and need? How can you add value to deliver those products/services to help their business grow?

- **Stakeholders:** What matters to them? How can you and your team meet their expectations?

- **Employees:** What do your employees need from you? How do you develop, motivate, improve collaboration, and reduce employee turnover?

- **Organization:** What are the organization, company, or industry's needs? How can your team contribute more to the organization? How can you lead your team to align and execute the company's strategy? What role can you and your team play to make a difference? Ask your management team these types of questions. Prepare yourself. Learn to read and understand the company's financial statements. Sit in on the investor relations quarterly calls. You'll be growing and developing as a strategic thinker. And you will be able to contribute value to the management conversations.

Be sure to check with your audience to make sure that you are on point as to what they value.

- What is the need?

- What are the expectations of the people you serve?

- What services can you provide that are most needed?

Identifying your strengths is an important part of the leadership brand, but the starting point is understanding what the people you serve expect from you. Once you clarify what is expected of you, the next step is to determine your top strengths that will help you to meet your audience's needs.

Identifying your strengths is an important
part of the leadership brand, but the
starting point is understanding what the
people you serve expect from you

Step 2: What Do You Want to be Known for?

What are those key attributes that you rely on to deliver results? When developing a leadership brand, focus on your professional, technical, and leadership skills that others perceive as strengths.

There are several ways to determine your key attributes:

1. Reflect back to situations where you were really good at doing something and it came easy for you. What were those skills?

2. Take an assessment like Myers Briggs or the DiSC personality assessment.

3. Take an assessment like StrengthsFinder. StrengthsFinder breaks up its list of thirty-four strengths into four domains of strengths: Executing Strengths, Influencing Strengths, Relationship Building Strengths, and Strategic Thinking Strengths.

4. Ask your manager, direct reports, peers, colleagues, and customers for feedback. How would they describe you as a leader? For example, would they describe you as collaborative, inclusive, innovative, strategic, tactical, subject-matter-expert, solution-driven, resilient, results-oriented?

Based on the purpose you want to achieve, narrow this list of descriptors in the following chart down to six to eight descriptors that best describe you, are needed to provide value to your target audience, and are critical to helping you achieve your purpose and move forward in your leadership role.

Accountable	Action-oriented	Adaptable	Advocate
Approachable	Agile	Analytical	Assertive
Builds collaborative teams	Builds relationships	Business acumen	Catalyst
Change agent	Charismatic	Coach and develop	Collaborative
Committed	Communicator	Compassionate	Competent
Confident	Conflict resolution	Connector	Conscientious
Consistent	Courage	Creative	Curious
Customer-focused	Cutting-edge	Decision maker	Decisive
Dedicated	Delegate	Deliberate	Dependable
Determined	Difference maker	Diplomatic	Disciplined
Drives results	Effective	Efficient	Emotional Intelligence
Enabler	Enthusiastic	Executes	Flexible

Focused	Foster teamwork	Game-changer	Listens
Inclusive	Influence	Innovator	Insightful
Inspires	Integrative	Integrity	Interpersonal Savvy
Intuitive	Inventive	Knowledgeable	Logical
Mediator	Mentor	Negotiator	Optimistic
Organized	Passionate	Persistent	Planner
Political Savvy	Prepared	Proactive	Problem Solver
Progressive	Quality-oriented	Relationship Management	Resilient
Responsive	Results-driven	Risk taker	Self-awareness
Self-confident	Servant leader	Sets new direction	Solutions driven
Straightforward	Strategic thinker	Strategist	Takes ownership
Talent leader	Teamwork	Time management	Trendsetter
Trustworthy	Values diversity	Values driven	Visionary leader

Once you have picked your six to eight descriptors, share them with your manager, peers, colleagues, and trusted subordinates. Ask them if those descriptors are what someone in a leadership role like yours should exhibit. If they are not, ask what descriptors they would use to describe what characteristics someone in a leadership role like yours should exhibit. This is a very useful exercise.

Step 3: What is unique about your approach?

For illustrative purposes only, once you have selected those six to eight descriptors and validated them with feedback from your team, use them to reflect your unique approach. You can also combine descriptors to create more powerful descriptions that define your uniqueness. For example, some combined descriptors could be:

- Deliberately collaborative
- Strategically results-oriented
- Independently innovative
- Solutions-driven talent leader

Step 4: What is the reason you do all of this?

Leaders must deliver results. So, think about these things: What is the impact your unique value can bring to your audience? And what is the outcome that you want to achieve?

List key accomplishments that demonstrate that you can do this. For example, my coaching client, Judi, said that the reason she does this is so that she can continue to deliver year-to-year financial results for the business and her key stakeholders.

Step 5: Putting it all together!

Let's pull everything together to create your brand statement. It is important to make the "so that" connection between what you want to be known for (Step 2) and your desired results/outcome (Step 4). Be sure to identify your audience and their needs.

There is no right or wrong way to write your personal leadership brand. You may decide to use two-word phrases, or you may just use one-word descriptors. It's a personal choice.

Here are three examples:

- I am an innovative, collaborative, and strategic leader focused on providing cutting-edge solutions for my client. I am known for creating high-performing teams that consistently deliver profitable sales to the organization. I am passionate about achieving a high level of customer satisfaction.

- I am a solutions-driven talent leader who develops talent to successfully achieve the organization's professional and business goals. I do this to optimize talent business results in a more efficient way.

- I am a results-driven leader committed to building, maintaining, and managing key strategic third-party vendor relationships to achieve business results. I do this by setting direction, leveraging resources, and delivering on aggressive goals with minimum risk. As a trusted partner, I work across levels to motivate and engage the inclusive team to support the organization's objectives.

Step 6: Test it!

Use this checklist to validate your personal leadership brand:

- Does this brand identity best represent who I am and what I can do?

- Will this brand identity create value in the eyes of the organization and key stakeholders?

- Can I live this brand? Can I incorporate these qualities into my day-to-day behavior? This requires practice.

Remember, your brand should evolve over time and change as you take on new levels of leadership. By implementing this process, you will feel more confident in communicating your value.

The next step is to communicate your personal leadership brand so everyone knows the value you bring to the organization.

Step 7: Create a tagline.

I always encourage my clients to create a short phrase that summarizes their brand statement. These statements are short and quickly define what you want to be known for. Think of an image or a catchy phrase that depicts the core of your leadership brand.

I recommend that you take your descriptors from your personal leadership brand and use them as these short taglines. For example, when you lead with "I'm a change agent" or "I'm a solution-driven talent leader," people will want to know more. It often leads to a conversation where you can communicate your full leadership brand.

Jo Miller, the author of *Woman of Influence: 9 Steps to Build Your Brand, Establish Your Legacy, and Thrive* has 100 Leadership Brand statements which are short one-liners. She divides the brands into five categories: Change Leader Brands, People Leader Brands, Results Leader Brands, Service Leader Brands, and Thought Leader Brands.[5] I really like this list of descriptors. You can use them in your personal leadership brand statement.

For example:

- *Change Leader Brands* include taglines such as transformational strategist, process improvement champion, a catalyst for change, transformer, and quiet organizer.

- *People Leader Brands* include transformational people catalyst, culture shifter, and fearless leader.

- *Results Leader Brands* include enabler, influencer and motivator, game changer, problem-solver, closer of big business deals, and leader who produces top-line growth.

- *Service Leader Brands* include customer-centric thinker, advocator, brand advocate, deliverer of delightful consumer experiences, and leader of change inspired by customers.

- *Thought Leader Brands* include trend-setter, innovator who creates winning strategies, negotiation strategist, innovation architect, perspective shifter, and visionary product leader.

Based on your brand statement, what category do you fall into? What is the short phrase that describes your leadership brand?

Communicate Your Personal Leadership Brand

Once you've developed your personal leadership brand, it is important to communicate the value you bring. You can turn this into an elevator speech and use it as the basis for bios, resumes, and social media summaries for developing a distinguishable and repeatable story.

At the beginning of this section, we talked about the importance of cultivating an online presence to broadcast your value to your network. No one will know what you are doing unless you take ownership and put it out there. The best way to reach your audience is to identify two to three platforms your audience frequents and then post regularly. Some of the platforms include LinkedIn, Facebook, Instagram, X (formerly Twitter), YouTube, Pinterest, Snapchat, and TikTok.

In addition to cultivating your online presence, it is important to establish and participate in both internal and external professional networking organizations. Women often look at networking to help others, whereas men often use networking for business purposes with specific outcomes in mind. Gain clarity on your reason for networking and how you plan to achieve your networking goals.

> No one will know what you are doing unless
> you take ownership and put it out there.

Once you have your personal leadership brand and can communicate it well, the next step is to begin to think more strategically about your career and develop the skills needed to close the gap.

CHAPTER FIVE

Think More Strategically about Your Career

If you don't know exactly where you're going,
how will you know when you get there?
—Steve Maraboli, Life, the Truth, and Being Free

To think more strategically about your career, you need a plan of action designed to help you achieve long-term goals and grow into your future role. It requires being aware of existing barriers and anticipating potential barriers, and then developing a strategy to overcome them.

Carla Harris, author of Lead to Win: How to Be a Powerful, Impactful, Influential Leader in Any Environment says, "When the opportunity to lead presents itself, it's too late to start to prepare. Whether it's taking leadership classes, taking on stretch assignments or projects, or reading books like this one, do what you need to be ready when the door opens."[6]

This is the model I coach my clients on when we talk about how to think more strategically about their careers. Focus on the barriers to growing your career, and put a strategic career plan in place to overcome those barriers. Let's talk about these things in more detail.

Step 1: Be Strategic

In my culture, we were raised to believe that if we worked hard and achieved our objectives, we would be recognized for our accomplishments. Nothing could have been further from the truth in my competitive sales environment. Napoleon Hill, the author of *Think and Grow Rich,* said, "You are the master of your destiny. You can influence, direct, and control your own environment. You can make your life what you want it to be."[7]

Marshall Goldsmith, author of *What Got You Here Won't Get You There,*[8] addresses the fact that many professionals get stuck at a certain level of success. For instance, they manage to climb to a middle-management position at their organization but always get passed over for promotion to the executive level.

Your hard work is paying off. You are doing well in your field. But there is something standing between you and the next level of achievement. Marshall talks about understanding what is holding you back and changing those behaviors to be able to advance to the next level of leadership.

What's holding you back? This is why it is so important to think more strategically about your career vs. putting it in the hands of others to decide your destiny. You have your best interest at heart.

Step 2: Be Your Own Cheerleader

In order to be your best advocate, you have to be confident. Confidence is complicated for women in the workplace. If you have too little confidence, the boss second-guesses your work. If you have too much confidence, your co-workers label you as bossy or not a team player. You're in a vicious circle not knowing how your actions will be received.

I maintain that confidence isn't really the problem. Most of us know that we are competent at our jobs. And confidence and ambition grow over time. But what causes us to doubt ourselves has to do with many of the things mentioned in the Leadership Signature section—a communication issue, a competency issue, a cultural issue, or a lack of feedback. After all, we are human. When you continuously get beat down, you will start to question yourself.

When I was in the sales organization, each month the management team recognized the sales and technical sales representatives, leaving me shocked and confused as to why I was not recognized. Nonetheless, I congratulated those who were recognized and began to talk to them to learn more about what they did to get the recognition.

Throughout those discussions, a message hit me repeatedly: *they were promoting themselves.* They were their best advocates. As I stated earlier, I was taught not to boast, to just do your job and your good work will be recognized. How could I boast and remain true to myself? I needed a plan where my clients and team members would willingly acknowledge my contributions.

Prior to each customer installation, I decided to ask my clients about their expectations to ensure they viewed our job as essential to a successful installation for their company. A checklist was created for what they wanted. At the completion of the installation, I would sit down with them to review the checklist. If they were happy, I would ask them to share their feedback with my management team. I even offered to draft a letter for them since I knew they had busy schedules. Most of the time, they said, "Thank you, I'd appreciate that." This gave me an opportunity to include all the things I did to ensure a satisfied client. Moreover, I was able to leverage my happy clients to share my good work and expertise with my management team. This turned out to be a winning strategy.

Be your own cheerleader! Learning to advocate for oneself is critical. It's an essential survival tool. People who are skilled at self-promotion receive more opportunities and chances in their careers than people who don't. Advocating for yourself becomes even more important as you move up the leadership chain.

Step 3: Know Your Worth

Self-advocacy is about more than confidence. It's about knowing your worth and making it known. When you know your worth, you feel more confident negotiating. Negotiating is a key skill you need in your toolbox. It's often uncomfortable to do but is needed for discussions around compensation and when you have to negotiate in the workplace.

- Use resources like Glass Door, salary.com, and PayScale to find out what you're worth. This will help strengthen your case if you are negotiating compensation.

- Try journaling. Keep a list of your career goals and write down any self-limiting beliefs you hold about your role and what leadership is "supposed" to look like for women. Recognize those biases and move past them. Share your achievements with your managers, trusted peers, and friends outside work. These things will help you improve your feelings of self-worth.

- Set boundaries and learn to say "no" or how to say, "This is a great opportunity, but it's more responsibility, so let's talk about how to make it a win-win situation for both of us."

* And, finally, *practice, practice, practice*. Get comfortable speaking up and being an advocate for yourself, especially when you are negotiating a new job or salary. All they can say is "no." But, for sure, you'll never know unless you ask.

Step 4: Take Responsibility for a Budget That Generates a Profit

According to a recent MIT study, women are less likely than men to be promoted. One reason why is that, although women receive higher performance ratings than their male colleagues, their "potential" ratings are typically lower.

The study found that *potential* is the driver behind promotions, and because of this discrepancy, women are 14% less likely to receive a promotion than their male counterparts. For women of color, the numbers are even bleaker.[9]

There are many biases contributing to these statistics. However, in my experience, understanding and managing budget, also known as profit-and-loss (P&L), can be a major contributor to helping you make a career jump. It isn't about knowing the numbers; it's about having strategic responsibility for those numbers and using them to prove your value and support your arguments.

I learned this when I led the Global Learning organization and had responsibility for one of the fastest-growing products in IBM, the mid-range product line. At the end of the year, I was really proud of my team's accomplishments. I far exceeded all of my peers when it came to the profit that we contributed to the business. I remember going into my manager's office for my year-end review, knowing I had earned a "far exceeded" the requirements of the job.

Michael congratulated me and then told me that my performance rating was that I "exceeded" the requirements of the job. I politely listened and told him that my team *far exceeded* the requirements of the job. After a few minutes, he told me to bring him the business case. I was happy to do that, although he should have known because he reaped the benefits as well.

I came back, reviewed my accomplishments with him, and walked out of his office with a "far exceeded" rating. He could not justify giving me anything other than that. I think he just assumed I would not challenge the status quo. What about you? *Are you challenging the status quo when you need to?*

Use your financial knowledge and accomplishments to increase your influence across the organization, and to persuade others, including your manager, that your work deserves to be recognized. To prove your value, you can put together a spreadsheet outlining in quantitative terms how your individual projects and successes contributed to the organization's goals and revenue objectives.

> What about you? *Are you challenging the status quo when you need to?*

Step 5: Your Support Team - Coaches, Mentors, & Sponsors

Have you ever had a career conversation with your manager about your next steps only to be told you have to *perform* at that level before you can be promoted? I did. Interestingly enough, this was never communicated to me beforehand. I didn't even *know* the job description for the next job, so how was I supposed to perform at the next level?

This hurdle seems to be commonplace for women. Research shows that, unlike women, men are not asked to perform at the next level in order to be promoted. An MIT Sloan study finds female employees are less likely to be promoted than their male counterparts, despite outperforming them and being less likely to quit.[10] So, why are women held to a higher standard than men, constantly having to prove their abilities in a way that men do not? Could it be that they are judged as having a lower leadership potential than men?

"What is commonly talked about in terms of management potential are characteristics such as assertiveness, executive skills, charisma, leadership, ambition."[11] These skills are highly subjective and stereotypically associated with male leaders, indicating a strong bias against women in assessments of potential.

In *Bias Interrupted,* Joan Williams outlines five forms of biases that are common in the workplace. One of these biases, called the "prove-it-again bias," shows how disadvantaged groups continuously have to prove themselves in a way that advantaged groups do not.[12]

White men tend to get by on their "potential," whereas people like me who are less privileged by their race and gender must constantly prove themselves in order to get ahead. For even the most ambitious women, making it to the top can be a steep ladder to climb and is often an out-of-reach goal. Having to always prove yourself is quite tiring. I faced this battle myself, and it ended up being a major reason why I finally left IBM.

A lack of support and commitment from company leaders for changing the disparity of male-to-female promotions allows this problem to continue. Leaders need to be proactive in redefining potential and providing support systems where women can get promoted.

At this stage of your leadership journey, you need the right resources and support people to help you build and shape your career. You may have heard leadership groups mention your needing a coach, having mentors, and cultivating relationships with sponsors. These are all valuable resources that can help you progress in your career. Let's discuss what they do and how they can help you on your leadership journey.

> Leaders need to be proactive in redefining potential and providing support systems where women can get promoted.

Coach

A coach is someone who will challenge you by asking powerful questions that take you deep inside yourself to uncover what's keeping you stuck. Coming face to face with your limiting beliefs and recognizing the reason that you are stuck—what's holding you back—often helps a person to move forward. There are a number of different specialties in the coaching field. If you want to become a more effective leader, seek out a Leadership coach. They are more focused on management and leadership skills (such as building high-performance teams).

Overall, coaching is more holistic because it embraces all areas of life and the person as a whole. It provides non-judgmental feedback. After a coaching conversation, you should be able to clearly identify the obstacles you need to overcome in order to get "unstuck."

Mentor

A mentor listens, provides insight, and shares their experience, knowledge, and connections. Typically, they come from a similar industry, geography, or career background and focus on professional development, guiding the mentee to achieve success in their job and offering advice based on their lived experiences.

They should be someone you can tell the truth to and be totally transparent with. You want to be able to be honest with them whether you are excelling or messing up. A mentor is someone that you can share the good, the bad, and the ugly with.

In looking for a mentor, know your long- and short-term goals. Whose job would you like to have in the next five or ten years? Who is in your existing network that can be your mentor or introduce you to someone?

The mentor can be internal or external to the organization. If they are external to the organization, it is important for them to understand the context or culture in which you are playing so they can tailor their advice to not only you, but also to the context or culture of the organization that you are in.

Sponsor

A sponsor is your cheerleader behind closed doors, using their influence to advocate on your behalf. A sponsor is someone who gives advice and provides guidance to help you navigate your career. They use their influence to advocate for you and to help you promote your career.

A sponsor is someone who believes in you and will take your name into the room. Behind closed doors, they will argue as to why you should lead a major initiative, be promoted into an executive position, get that top bonus, or be the next global leader. They have political capital, are well respected, and make things happen. A sponsor is a person that you always let see you in a positive light so they will champion you. Whereas a mentor sees your good, bad, and ugly, your sponsor should only see your good, better, and best!

Finding a sponsor is not as direct as finding a mentor or coach. You need to be intentional in your search for a sponsor. Look around the organization for people who have achieved your goals and who are where you would like to be. Join some networking groups where influential people are involved. Look for someone who is in a position with real power to change your career.

Once you have identified that senior leader who can help you in your career, take the initiative to make yourself visible. Get involved, take on projects, speak up with your ideas in meetings, and make connections. Develop a relationship with them. Ask for feedback and guidance. If they see you taking their advice, they will be more inclined to champion you.

This is a two-way street. You must bring value to the sponsor. By helping them achieve their own objectives, they will notice your contribution and realize that you have the potential to do more. Promote yourself and let people know what you are doing. You will earn the right by performing well and building a solid reputation for doing what you say you will do and for successfully delivering results. If someone is going to put their reputation on the line, they need to trust you and know that you will not let them down.

Though women are often provided mentors and coaches, sponsors must be earned. This is the most important relationship to have with respect to advancing within the organization.

All three of these resources are valuable in helping you grow as a leader and advance to the next level. My advice is to have all three. Ask for a coach and a mentor and set yourself apart from the others so you will become more visible and increase your chances of getting a sponsor.

Step 6: Executive Presence

Have you ever noticed someone who walks into a room and just owns it? That was my dad, Rev. R.W. Stallings. He was a man of small stature, but when he walked into a room, you could hear him throughout the entire room.

He "worked" the room. He would go up to everyone to shake their hands, laughing and making them feel comfortable. He was known as the little man with the firm handshake. He always had something special to say to each person to make them feel important. When he laughed, the whole room heard him. And he was always decked out in a suit, white shirt, matching tie, and wing-tip shoes. That's who he was.

I remember years later when I was in high school, I tried to convince my dad that he didn't have to wear a white shirt every day. But that white shirt was part of his professional appearance whether he went to church or a family picnic. It was who he was.

I can think of several people I know who have that Executive Presence. They are confident and comfortable in their own skin. They are friendly, warm, and welcoming. Their appearance is put together with everything in place and dressed appropriately for the occasion. As they walk around the room, it's clear they have excellent communication and interpersonal skills, making everyone feel seen and heard. They are positive and optimistic, and when they speak, it is with authority. They seem to have quite a bit of influence and impact.

Executive Presence is one of those things that is hard to put into words. In its simplest terms, Executive Presence is about your ability to inspire confidence among your peers, colleagues, and subordinates. And, most importantly, it's about inspiring confidence that you are capable and reliable. It is when your senior leaders believe that you have the potential.

Executive Presence can be described as:

- Creating the **mindset** that you can do it. It's about having control over yourself and believing that you can lead, which is known as self-efficacy. A good example of this is what Muhammad Ali did. He began telling the world that he was the greatest heavyweight boxer at a time when he wasn't. But, over time, he became ranked as one of the greatest boxers of all time.

- The ability to **communicate** with words and actions in a way that inspires others to follow.

- A combination of **behaviors and attitudes** that enable you to express your ideas and influence others clearly and confidently. Authenticity, confidence, competence, and trustworthiness are all important aspects of a strong Executive Presence.

- How you carry yourself in a **professional manner**. It is your actions, which speak louder than words. Do you hold up well under fire? Are you dependable? Are you accountable? Do you keep your word? Are you emotionally intelligent when working with others? All of these things make up Executive Presence.[13]

The measure of a person's Executive Presence is the extent to which people will listen and give weight to what the person says. Are you able to effectively encourage people to listen and inspire them to act? Executive presence is a skill you cultivate and build with focus and practice.

Why Does Executive Presence Matter?

The impression you make on the people you work with matters. Executive presence shows others you are a talented professional capable of leading others and making meaningful contributions to the company. It determines whether you gain access to opportunities (promotions, critical roles, leading highly visible assignments/initiatives), get on that high-potential list, or get a sponsor. Have you inspired the trust and confidence in the decision-makers? The more significant the opportunity, the more important Executive Presence becomes.

Executive presence shows others you are a talented professional capable of leading others and making meaningful contributions to the company.

When I work with leaders who want me to coach their employees, they describe Executive Presence in so many different ways. Thom described Anne, saying, "When she does a presentation, she does a good job; however, she can't think on her feet." Susan described Latisha as, "Rambling and looking uncomfortable when she responds to questions." Brittany described Linda as being, "Too laid back and not being able to read people." All of these things relate to how people perceive you—Executive Presence.

The way you present yourself sends a message to everyone around you. You must be aware of your appearance and body language. You must also possess the ability to understand facial expressions and nonverbal communication.[14] If you only listen to what a person says and ignore what their face is telling you, then you really won't get the whole story. Often, words do not match emotions; it's the face that betrays what a person is actually feeling.

One of my biggest challenges has always been that my facial gestures show how I really feel. Being conscious of this has always been a challenge for me. Not being able to control my facial gestures could convey to someone that I think they have a "dumb idea" or that I don't understand or agree with what they are saying. I've always admired my peers who could have a poker face and not show any emotions. Nonverbal messages through facial expressions convey a lot that words do not.

Key Steps to Build Executive Presence

In order to build Executive Presence, it is important to understand the barriers to career growth. A Forbes article on Executive Presence identified several key areas to focus on that will help you build and enhance Executive Presence.[15]

- **Have a vision and communicate it well.** When you have a vision, you know what you're working to accomplish. Gaining clarity on your vision will help you become more confident when communicating with your team, senior executives, or stakeholders. For some people, it's having an elevator pitch. I always recommend taking the time to develop a personal leadership brand statement as it is one tool to help develop your vision and communicate it effectively. What is your vision?

- **Understand how others experience you.** As you move up to more senior-level roles and your span of control expands, you become even more reliant on others for your effectiveness. But before you get access to the more senior opportunities, decision-makers need to be confident that you can handle yourself well in all settings and situations.

  Take the time to understand how others perceive you because perception is reality. Are you approachable, credible, competent, and relatable? Do they find you trustworthy? If you have not created your personal leadership brand statement, this is a good time to get feedback from your manager, mentors, peers, and subordinates relative to how they experience you, then put in the work to close the skill gaps.

- **Learn how to communicate more effectively.**
Communicating clearly and effectively is one of the most critical components of Executive Presence. How you communicate determines your ability to influence and inspire others. Good leadership is about communication, and people who have Executive Presence are excellent communicators.

Have you ever talked on the phone to someone, and then when you meet them, they do not look anything like what you pictured in your mind? So many times, people tell me, "I thought you were taller," or "You're a little person."

Your voice projects an image of strength or weakness. It also communicates biases through our word choices and how we frame our questions. How you talk contributes a big part to your personal presence.

As leaders, we have to balance authority, credibility, and likeability. Yes, it's challenging to do that, but look at it another way; it's an opportunity to learn how to master communications which will make you a stronger and more effective leader. How do you show up?

Make sure your message is concise and well-suited to your audience. For example, a busy executive is likely to appreciate a "just the facts" approach, while someone new to their position may appreciate context and detail. Being an excellent communicator across every medium—in person, written, or virtually—and in every situation is a critical skill to Executive Presence.

- **Become an excellent listener.** Your ability to listen is an important communication skill. People with Executive Presence are exceptional listeners. They engage, focus, are curious, and ask great questions.

  Excellent listeners use listening to engage others and explore ideas. Listen to understand what the other person is saying rather than just trying to jump in with your comment. When you listen to understand, you will gain a better understanding of what's important to the other person and have the opportunity to explore possibilities that are amiable for both parties.

  The ability to listen effectively demonstrates self-confidence, which is a critical part of Executive Presence.

- **Learn how to operate effectively under stress.** Your thought process is often challenged during a crisis, in a meeting when people are tossing out ideas, when you are responding to challenging questions, or when you are called on unexpectedly and have to respond. People watch how you respond and form opinions about how well you handle situations.

  How do you react under pressure? Do you appear overwhelmed or flustered? Do you have a reputation for being temperamental? Many people make the mistake of believing that looking "busy" indicates how valuable you are to the organization. But in certain scenarios, it can send the message that you are out of control, overwhelmed, or that you can't handle more responsibility.

  When you have Executive Presence, you present yourself as calm, composed, well-prepared, and in control. This presence shows senior management that you're ready to take on even more responsibility.

- **Make sure your appearance isn't a distraction.** Your physical presence makes a first impression, and first impressions are memorable and powerful. Physical appearance, including body language, voice, and physical movement, counts for connections, persuasion, engagements, and credibility.

When you interact with someone who has Executive Presence, they look you in the eye when they speak and have a firm handshake. How you project yourself physically shapes your impact among your colleagues. If you are uncomfortable projecting an image of confidence and power, get comfortable with it! It is essential to stand in your power.

Make sure that your appearance is appropriate for the setting and the company culture, and that it is consistent with others at the level to which you aspire. Choose your clothing wisely. Make sure there is nothing about your appearance that will distract those you are trying to impress.

- **Cultivate your network and build political savvy.** Be it good or bad, organizational politics exist. The more you create opportunities to grow your network, the more you grow your resources, support team, and open up opportunities to grow.

A special note on your Executive Presence in a **virtual environment**: More organizations are embracing virtual meeting platforms, and remote work is slowly becoming the norm for many people. Cultivating your Executive Presence is just as important in a virtual environment as it is in the physical office. Some points to remember include:

- Be engaged. Keep your camera on to convey that you are present. Avoid distractions like email and your phone.

- Manage your lighting. Try to sit in a well-lit area and position yourself so that the windows are in front of you rather than behind you to avoid a shadow.

- Be aware of your background. Make sure it is clean and clutter-free.

- Check your camera angles. Position the camera so your face is centered in the middle, and you have eye-level contact. You may have to look up at the camera to make sure that you are looking at your audience.

- Consider your clothing. Finally, choose to wear colors that are solid with high contrast.

Executive Presence is that special sauce that makes you stand out. It makes you credible, respectable, and trustworthy. Executive Presence takes time to develop, but it is an important skill if you want to grow as a leader.

Assess yourself. Which of these seven steps do you need to develop? Make a list of them. In the next and final section, you will create a plan to close these skill gaps.

Knowledge Matters

After you gain clarity on your leadership signature (who you are), have written your personal leadership brand statement, and have assessed which Executive Presence skills you need to develop/enhance, the next step is to assess your current skills and the skills you need to develop in order to achieve your vision.

Knowing your skills and talents facilitates personal growth. Focusing on your strengths can help you achieve your goals and give you greater confidence. For example, if you are asked to join the swim team, and you know that you are not a strong swimmer, nor do you want to spend the time and energy to improve, you might decide not to do it.

That's similar to a job in the workplace. If you are an extrovert and love to talk to people, you would go crazy sitting in an office coding all day long and vice versa. When you focus on your talents and the things you enjoy, you are happier and more productive.

Craft a Strategic Career Plan

Now that you understand the barriers to career growth and how to grow into your future role, you are ready to develop a strategic career plan to take you to the next level. Creating a strategic career plan requires that you identify the competency and skill areas that you need in order to remove barriers to your career growth.

Determine your Competencies

To begin, if your company has an option for you to take a 360 assessment, take it. It will help to spotlight your strengths and your areas for development. If your company does not provide this option, there are other ways you can determine the skills/

competencies that you need to develop by doing a self-initiated feedback survey.

In the personal leadership brand section, we talked about the option of doing a self-initiated feedback survey. If you decide to do one, identify six to eight people you work with to give you feedback. Again, this can be your manager, direct reports, peers, stakeholders, senior management, colleagues, etc.

Send them an email briefly explaining that your objective is to gain feedback to help in your development as a leader. Let them know that you value their feedback. If they agree to meet with you, send them a short list of questions to prepare. You may want to ask them what they consider to be your strengths, areas for development, and how they would describe you as a leader.

Summarize the feedback from all respondents, focusing on the common themes, the skills to improve, and which skill gaps to close.

Once you have honestly assessed your competencies and determined which competencies you plan to focus on for improvement, it's time to create your goals. I often recommend using the SMART goals template for my clients.

SMART is an acronym used to describe the process of setting goals. It stands for:

Specific—a description of what must be done and by whom.

Measurable—a description of how success will be measured.

Achievable—is the goal consistent with business goals, objectives, and strategy.

Relevant—is the goal challenging enough to justify doing it?

Time-bound—can the goal be accomplished within the timeframe?

It provides a way to measure your progress on your goals. It allows you to determine what you are trying to achieve and set actionable tactics to reach those goals. However, if you have another process that is more effective for you, use it.

Here's an example of a more simplified SMART template:

Goal	Outcome: What Success Looks Like	Tactic (Steps to achieve goal)	Completion date

Set your goals!

In setting your goals, use action verbs like *lead, implement, build, demonstrate, influence, drive,* etc.

What does success look like?

Once you set your goals, determine what success looks like. In other words, how will you evaluate if you were successful in achieving your goals?

What are the actionable steps to achieve your goals?

Next, identify all the short-term tactical things you need to do to bridge the gap between where you are and where you want to be. Tactics may include tapping into resources, increasing learning, engaging in activities, volunteering to do presentations, leading a work effort, and shadowing to help improve the identified gaps in capabilities and skills.

Set due dates to hold yourself accountable.

Finally, after you have identified each goal and tactic, determine due dates to complete each goal and task. Due dates are effective in that they hold you accountable for achieving the goal or task.

After you develop your plan, keep it in front of you. Post it somewhere where you see it. Make it a priority and check it each month. Update it, as needed. This will be a valuable tool to help you achieve your goals.

In summary, this chapter has provided you with ideas, suggestions, and action steps to make yourself a high-potential leader. And yes, leaders need to be at the absolute top of their personal game, no question.

However, leadership doesn't happen in a vacuum. Interacting with and successfully supporting a team is also necessary. Companies want to know that you are a team leader, team player and are respected and trusted by the organization.

In the next section, It's About the People, we will talk more about your role as a leader and how to be more effective and impactful in leading others.

SECTION ONE
KEY TAKEAWAYS

1. Your Leadership Signature is like your personal name
    signature or your thumbprint. It is what you bring to
    the table that differentiates you. Your unique Leadership
    Signature is made up of three primary components–
    your uniqueness, your self-efficacy, and your credibil-
    ity. Defining this uniqueness and being comfortable
    with who you are will help you to "***stand in your
    authenticity***!"

2. A personal leadership brand communicates your unique
    selling proposition by defining who you are as a leader,
    what you value, and what differentiates you from your
    competition. It is based on your beliefs, your work and
    life experiences, your personality, and your desire to
    have an impact on your business, your stakeholders,
    and society at large. It is designed the same way that
    one develops a brand statement for a product, service,
    or company. Defining your personal leadership brand
    will help you to "***step into your power.***"

3. To help you achieve long-term goals and grow into your
    future role, you must be aware of existing barriers and
    anticipate potential barriers, then develop a strategy
    to overcome them. This will help you to "***think more
    strategically about your career.***" This requires that you:
    *   Be strategic—focus on the skills and behaviors to
        advance you to the next level.
    *   Be your own cheerleader.

- Know your worth
- Understand and manage budget (P&L).
- Have your support team—a coach, mentor, and sponsor.
- Develop Executive Presence

4. You can build and enhance Executive Presence by focusing on these seven key areas:
   - Have a vision and communicate it well.
   - Understand how others experience you.
   - Learn how to communicate more effectively.
   - Become an excellent listener.
   - Learn how to operate effectively under stress.
   - Make sure your appearance isn't a distraction.
   - Cultivate your network and build political savvy.

5. A strategic career plan will help you focus on the skills needed to advance to the next level. When crafting a strategic career plan, you must determine your needs, set your goals, identify tactical steps to achieve those goals, and set due dates to hold yourself accountable.

IT'S ABOUT THE PEOPLE

It is literally true that you can succeed best
and quickest by helping others to succeed.
—Napoleon Hill

Making the transition from an individual contributor to a first-time people leader can be quite challenging. Marshall Goldsmith summed it up eloquently with the title of his book: *What Got You Here Won't Get You There*. So true!

Most people think that because they were outstanding individual contributors, they will be outstanding and effective leaders of people. This is not necessarily the case, as I experienced firsthand when Bill became my manager.

Bill was a great technical subject matter expert (SME). When he was promoted from another department and became our manager, he thought that he could continue doing the individual contributor job *and* his new job as manager. What we ended up with was a micromanager. Bill did not trust that we could do the job, so he was involved in every decision. It was awful, to the point I transferred to another department. *What a relief!*

You see, being a leader of people requires a different set of skills and competencies—many of which you may not have had to use before as an individual contributor. Some of these leadership skills include developing talent, delegating, coaching, building relationships, and leading teams. When you are an individual contributor, you are only responsible for your own performance. But when you become a manager, your success is based on the success of your team. So, the "Me" mindset has to become the "We" mindset.

Emotional intelligence is an intangible yet essential competency that must be a priority for all leaders. It enables leaders to understand and manage their own emotions effectively, fostering self-awareness, self- management, and social awareness. Additionally, leaders with high emotional intelligence can empathize with others, building strong relationships and cultivating a positive work environment. By effectively navigating emotions, leaders can inspire and motivate their teams, make sound decisions, and handle conflicts with empathy and tact, ultimately driving higher levels of employee engagement and organizational performance.

One of the first things I discuss with new managers is that they need to get comfortable with not having all of the answers. It's imperative to surround yourself with a competent team of individuals whose strengths are different from yours. When faced with a situation where you aren't sure of the answer, view it as an opportunity for growth rather than a moment of weakness. Ask your team for their input and let them know you value their expertise. If no one has the answer, simply seek out the answer and get back to them. You may be more comfortable saying, "Let me check the latest information on that, and I'll get back to you."

> One of the first things I discuss with new managers is that they need to get comfortable with not having all of the answers.

Thinking like a leader is a big part of being a leader. Adopting a leadership mindset of "what you don't know, you can find the resources to figure out" will serve you well as a leader.

In writing this section, "It's About the People," I wanted to include strategies and tools to help you effectively take on new leadership roles, regardless of whether you are a first-time manager or a seasoned manager. In this section, we will explore driving results by effectively leading change and transition. We will discuss how to become an agile leader, and how to embrace diverse and inclusive teams.

When I moved into a new leadership role, I dedicated the first ninety days to diving in, understanding the business, understanding my new role, getting to know the key players, and beginning to develop the talent—all with the end goal in mind to "drive results" in the organization.

Yes, I said my first *ninety days* because so many unforeseen and unanticipated situations pop up that it takes time to let them surface naturally. The timeframe isn't written in stone; the time it will take you depends on your experience and the type of situation that you are walking into. A good rule of thumb is somewhere in the neighborhood of ninety days.

CHAPTER SIX

Leading Change and Transition

Be the change you wish to see in the world.
—Mahatma Gandhi

Change is inevitable and is becoming the norm. Effectively leading change and transition is *not* inevitable. Leaders have no choice but to adapt and to help others to adapt, too.

As a leader, you set the example, and you play a major role in helping transition your team to your company's new vision. Change impacts employees at every level. A leader needs to understand their team's needs and how to inspire them to embrace shifting ideas. Change management doesn't work unless the leader understands how to be an effective leader. This is an essential skill.

Effective leaders understand how their emotions shape their thoughts and actions. They know that when there are changes happening in the structure or operations of the organization, it's important to pay attention to how people are feeling. This is called emotional intelligence.

People with high emotional intelligence can recognize their own feelings and the feelings of others. They can predict how their actions might affect others. Equally important, they understand the range of emotions and actions that may have influenced someone's decision.

They can use this understanding of emotions, both their own and others', to make decisions and take actions, knowing that different people will react in different ways. So, how can a leader improve their emotional intelligence and become more self-aware? One way is by understanding the business goals, building relationships, and getting to know the needs of their team and stakeholders.

If you are a first-time manager or a seasoned leader who is moving into a new role and want to be viewed as an impactful, influential, and effective leader, this section is for you. The first ninety days in a new position are critical because your actions can have a huge impact on the long-term results. It is important to understand the challenges and opportunities quickly.

Coming into a new role, this is your opportunity to listen and learn. You are entering new territory, so the first ninety days are your opportunity to ask a lot of questions to clarify and set yourself up for success. This is your learning phase and is often referred to as your grace period. People expect a new person to ask questions. However, if you have been in the job for a couple of years and you're asking some basic questions, people will question whether this is the right job for you.

Take in as much as you can during your learning phase.

- Seek input by listening more and talking less. Soak everything in like a sponge.

- Determine your learning gaps, then identify people you would consider to be critical resources who can bring you up to speed, and schedule time with them.

- Ask questions to find out what your area does well and what needs to be improved. What advice do they have?

- Identify critical meetings, committees, and teams in which you should participate.

There are three key areas that require your immediate attention—understanding the business objectives, uncovering the challenges, and developing key relationships. Let's take a look at each of these areas.

Understand the Business Objectives

As you begin to roll up your sleeves to understand the business, it is important to gain clarity on the reason you were brought into the organization. Were you brought in to revitalize the group and take it to the next level, realign the organization, change the organization's strategy, provide structure, develop skills, or even revitalize its corporate culture? Understand the underlying reasons. This should be discussed with your leader when you have a conversation relative to their expectations.

To understand the business, you must first recognize there are two areas to tackle. These are maintaining the momentum—keeping the business running—while at the same time clarifying the vision and strategy imperatives. Let's take a look at both of these.

To diagnose the business situation to determine the current situation, you first want to understand the problems. What major problems have you inherited? Perhaps it's strife within the team or within different departments. Or perhaps your team is not making their goals.

What is the root cause behind these problems? Start by asking questions and listening more than talking. Then meet with your manager to discuss what you observed, get your manager's feedback, and determine the next steps before taking any action to resolve the problems. If you aren't in agreement on how to resolve the issues, determine why, and figure out a way to effect a resolution.

Co-create with your leadership team the goals, objectives, and metrics for success, such as profitability, etc. Once you determine the key performance indicators (KPIs), put a plan in place to communicate them periodically to senior management. These KPIs will serve as quantifiable measures of performance over time for your specific strategic objectives. Create an action plan with timelines to ensure all team members agree and are on board relative to how to achieve the team's business objectives.

While learning all about the business, how to run it effectively, and identifying the key players that help to do so, you must still drive the business forward. Some ways that you can do this include:

- Clarify the mission and establish the vision and strategic initiatives.

- Conduct a business review to identify how to achieve business objectives.

- Identify critical issues that require immediate action and prioritize issues according to the organization's strategy.

Build Key Relationships

The success of an organization depends on how well its leaders collaborate. During the first thirty to sixty days in your new role, take the time to get to know and establish a relationship with key people in your organization:

Your Manager

The first place to develop a solid working relationship is with your manager. What are their professional and personal aspirations? What drives them? What are their pet peeves? How can you best support them?

Throughout my career, I always let my manager know I was there to make them look good. If they know I have their back, hopefully, they will have my back.

To establish a good relationship with your new manager, focus on these areas:

Performance goals:

- What are their key performance goals?
  - How do your performance goals align with theirs?
  - How will success be measured?
  - Have you gained clarity on what is expected?
  - What needs to be accomplished? By when?
  - What is the best way to accomplish those goals?
- *Leadership style:*
  - What is their leadership style?
- *Decision-making process/authority:*
  - When do they want you to check in with them?
  - Do they prefer you to check in first or complete the task and then let them know?

- *Communication style:*
  - ° What is their communication style?
  - ° How do they like to be updated?
  - ° How often?

- *Support:*
  - ° What support do you need to be successful and from whom (cross-functional, peers, HR, etc.).

- *Problems:*
  - ° What problems are your manager aware of within the team?
  - ° Were there any things that your predecessor did not accomplish that are high on your manager's list?

- *Team morale:*
  - ° What's the team's overall morale?
  - ° What has happened to cause the morale to be where it is?

- *Early wins:*
  - ° Are there any early wins you can make happen to enhance your credibility?
  - ° What are the early wins that matter to your management team?
  - ° How quickly do you need to create those early wins?

- *Timelines:*
  - ° What are the timelines—how quickly do these things need to be handled?

Your Stakeholders, Peers, and Colleagues

Next to your manager, it is important to begin to connect with your stakeholders, peers, and colleagues. Your stakeholders matter! They may have been influential in making that decision to bring you into the organization. And, if so, they will be influential in moving you out of the organization.

Your peers, colleagues, stakeholders, and senior management are all people that you will have to work with. The reality is, people feel comfortable around people they like. As I mentioned before, I thought that if I did my job, I would advance, but the reality is that networking, going out for drinks, and playing tennis and golf are all activities that help people to feel more comfortable around you.

> The reality is, people feel comfortable around people they like.

I cannot begin to tell you how many of my coaching clients that chose not to develop those relationships now regret that decision. As you advance in your career, the need to become more strategic and political becomes even more important to help you accomplish your goals. So, these key players should be high on your list to identify, develop relationships with and understand their needs.

As you identify the key players, ask yourself:

- Who are the leaders that have executive presence and are respected within the organization?
- Who has the formal power?
- Who has informal power?

- Who are the chosen few, the up-and-coming leaders within the organization?

- Who is viewed as less influential or perceived as "on the outs"?

- Who is leading the "hot" projects and initiatives?

- Who are the political players that you should not offend?

- And how will you engage people and gain buy-in support for the work that has to be done?

After identifying these key players, you should:

- Schedule introductory meetings to assess their needs and expectations.

- Create a plan for building critical relationships and map out a communication strategy across stakeholders.

- Prepare a "Business Review" to communicate your plans to achieve objectives to internal and external stakeholders and to gain visibility among the key stakeholders. When creating this review, determine: What does your organization do well? What needs to be improved? What does success look like to your stakeholders?

- Provide checkpoints to communicate periodically and to remain visible.

Your Direct Reports

Building credibility and trust with your direct reports is another key to your success. Trust is an essential part of building those relationships. A team will not be effective unless you build trust among the members.

Listening to what they have to say and acting on it is one way to build credibility and trust. Listening is a critical skill to learn. Meet with each of your leaders one-on-one to understand their business challenges, what's working, and what they need help with. Learn what motivates them, how they prefer to be recognized, their skill set, the areas they need to develop, and their personal goals. Encourage your leaders to ask questions and invite their input. Make them feel a part of the team and that their insight is valued. It is important to acknowledge and understand their point of view.

When it came to engaging with my team, my presence was always seen on the floor. It was an opportunity for me to find out what they were working on and to let them know that I was there if they needed any help. While in the office, my door was always open.

Don't be shy about getting to know your team on a personal level, too. It builds trust in the relationship to know that you care about what is happening to them outside of the office. If and when you can, help them with some of their personal goals as well as their professional ones. Let them know you have a personal interest in their success.

And don't forget relationships are two-way streets. Let them get to know you, as a person. Be comfortable with asking for feedback relative to your leadership style. Building strong relationships will also build your strength as a trusted influential leader.

Your HR Partner

To set yourself up for success in your new position, it is crucial to develop a strong relationship with your HR partner. Take the initiative to schedule a meeting with them to discuss their preferred engagement style and how they can support you. Tap into their knowledge of your functional area, the team dynamics, and the challenges you may face. Establish clear communication channels and timelines for reaching out to them.

Additionally, leverage their expertise in team-building exercises, such as using assessments like DiSC and Myers Briggs, to foster understanding and collaboration within your team. Consult with HR to gain insights into high-potentials and the successor process.

Lastly, stay proactive by noting key timelines and deadlines provided by HR and adding them to your calendar to ensure preparedness rather than being caught off guard in reactive mode.

CHAPTER SEVEN

Agile Leadership

*Success today requires the agility and drive to
constantly rethink, reinvigorate, react, and reinvent.*
—Bill Gates

Once you understand the business needs and have begun to develop key relationships, the next step is to develop your agile leadership capabilities. Agile leadership is about driving, promoting and being the change. Agile leaders lead by example and actively engage and inspire others by their actions.

Know the Capabilities of Your Team

As an agile leader, it is important to know the capabilities of your team so you can actively engage and inspire them. One way to do this is to assess the team's talent, both individually and collectively, and put plans in place to develop the team. This process will allow you to determine what capabilities, roles, and work processes are required to drive the strategic imperatives.

You can assess the individual capabilities of each of your direct reports against the organization's present and future business needs. Ask your leadership team questions like:

- What challenges do you currently face leading your team?

- What challenges do you anticipate?

- What areas would you like to improve on?

- What do you need from me to help make your job easier?

- What are the biggest challenges the organization is facing?

- What are the growth areas and opportunities for the organization?

- If you were me, what would you focus on?

Have your leadership team assess the capabilities of their direct reports against the present and future business needs. This will help you determine any skill gaps that may prevent you from achieving the business goals.

You also will want to assess the capabilities of your leadership team as a whole to determine if they are collectively ready to achieve present and future business results.

- Where are your leadership team's skill gaps?

- How can you close those gaps?

- Who are the high performers and high potential?

- Who are the mentors?

- Who are the subject matter experts (SMEs) and how can I best utilize them?

After talking with each team leader and assessing the individual and collective skills and skill gaps, you are in a better position to create a plan to achieve the business objectives.

Developing Talent

One of the biggest challenges a leader faces is in developing their people so they are capable of delivering the results the business needs. Today, it is even more difficult when your team can include different generations and cultures with different outlooks on what they want in a job or career.

There are several ways to develop an employee: training, stretch assignments, projects that allow your people to grow, and rotating jobs or tasks, which provides a wider range of skills and knowledge. It also helps them better understand how their work contributes to achieving organizational goals.

Developing talent gives them an opportunity to gain experience and to take on new jobs and responsibilities to set them up to be more competitive. I once had a manager who would not let me take a new opportunity simply because he did not have the foresight to train someone to backfill me. As a result, I was one unhappy high-performing team member and eventually left the organization.

It may seem counterintuitive to begin a new role by thinking about your successor, but it is absolutely the right time to do so, and to develop your team's talent with a succession plan in mind.

Always have your eye on the next position and do at least one thing a week to get closer to that next position. Have a plan for your career. It doesn't have to be a rigid plan but a guiding goal of what you want to achieve and by when. We get so caught up in the day-to-day activities that if you don't focus on that one big goal, you'll get stuck. If you know your next move, begin to develop the skills you need to be more impactful in that next role and demonstrate them in your current role.

I never lost sight of this in my new roles because I knew myself all too well—once I learned the job at hand, I began to look for my next challenge. In fact, this was something I spoke to my manager about coming into the job (and you should, too).

Ask how long they anticipate it would take you to achieve the goals they are hiring you for. This way, when you have helped them achieve their objectives and goals, you should be free to pursue your next career move within the organization.

Have you ever become aware of an excellent opportunity to advance your career, only to be told you couldn't move until you had a successor? For many, this is all too often the case, and leads to either stagnation within their current position or seeking employment outside of the organization.

Don't let the frustration of being held back due to the lack of a successor impede your progress. Proactively planning for succession empowers you to navigate your career path with confidence and seize new opportunities for advancement.

> Proactively planning for succession empowers you to navigate your career path with confidence and seize new opportunities for advancement.

Performance Management

There are various thoughts about whether or not organizations should utilize performance reviews to develop their teams' talent. I believe there should be a way to hold team members accountable, so I am a proponent of them.

Let me be clear: I do not advocate using performance reviews as a way to slam or shame a team member. Rather, I believe it helps a person to keep their focus on what matters. What are the objectives the organization is working toward achieving? Keep these objectives in sight.

As a leader, you are responsible for setting performance objectives or goals for each team member. This is one way to clearly communicate the results that need to be accomplished and what constitutes the expected levels of performance and successful professional development.

No matter what process your company uses, the bottom line is that the leader needs to provide each team member with their goals. In other words, how will they be measured? What are they expected to achieve by year-end?

When goals and objectives are identified, the next step is to determine the tactics. What are all of the tactical things that need to be completed? By when? Allow your people to take the initiative to develop their own tactics. This will be easier for the more seasoned team members; you will need to help the team members who are new to the job. Review their tactics with them, and offer suggestions where needed.

One of the biggest mistakes I see leaders make is to agree upon annual goals and objectives with their team members, and then never touch them again until it comes time for the year-end performance review. Leaders must provide feedback periodically through one-on-one meetings to discuss their progress.

I met with each leader quarterly. They would provide me with a recap of their accomplishments relative to their goals.

My expectations were that they would come to those quarterly meetings prepared to discuss what they had achieved year-to-date, what they have yet to achieve, any issues or problems, and where they could use my help. It was an opportunity to provide feedback and offer suggestions in a non-threatening conversation.

This was also an opportunity to communicate my view that just meeting the objectives means they have achieved "meets requirements" of the job. To achieve an "exceeds requirements" of the job, I would be looking for difference makers. For example, did they volunteer to help others? Did they assume a leadership role on the team? Did they mentor others?

Consider implementing quarterly or bi-annual interim reviews. I know this seems time-consuming, but there are new tools that can help you set up reviews quickly and more frequently.

At the end of the year, prior to our official performance evaluation meeting, I sent their performance review to them. As a result, when they walked into my office, they already knew their year-end rating. The purpose of our discussion was for them to recap the year, discuss lessons learned, and tell me what they would do differently next year.

This was my approach. Other organizations have different approaches to performance evaluation. One HR department I know uses an Artificial Intelligence (AI) tool. In the first quarter, the employees' objectives for the year are entered into the system. In the second quarter, they review how the objectives are coming along. The third quarter involves a career development discussion, and the fourth quarter is the year-end performance review.

Whatever the system or procedure, the main point to remember is to employ frequent touchpoints throughout the year.

Speaking of performance management, it is also important for you to gather feedback from others assessing your leadership qualities. You can do your own self-assessment or take a 360 assessment, where you can solicit feedback from your manager, direct reports, peers, and colleagues. With the 360-assessment process, you are able to:

- Understand others' impressions of how you lead day by day. Are you more people-focused or more task focused?

- How would they describe your leadership?

- What do they view as your strengths and development areas?

- Consider: Are you changing the culture? Are you driving results? If not, pivot and change your approach.

Utilizing performance reviews can be an effective way for leaders to hold team members accountable and ensure focus on organizational objectives. However, it is crucial to approach performance reviews as a constructive tool for professional development.

Regular feedback and touchpoints throughout the year, along with self-assessment and gathering feedback from others, contribute to a comprehensive performance management process that helps leaders improve their leadership qualities and drive positive change.

Strategically Delegating

Delegation is a key strategic skill that differentiates new managers from experienced managers. It's just not possible to be an experienced manager and not delegate. If you don't delegate, you won't have time for thinking strategically, which is a key skill to advance to the next level.

Did you know that the number-one derailer for leaders is overmanaging? This occurs when leaders micromanage by trying to control everything and not delegating enough. A leader's success depends on their team's performance. Failure to delegate is a sure formula for overload and burnout.

As women, we have worked so hard to get where we are. We are self-sufficient. We can do it all! You may feel that everyone is overworked, and you don't want to delegate it to anyone else, so you do it yourself.

Or, if you are like me, you may be a perfectionist. And we often feel that we don't want to let go and give the responsibility to someone else because they won't do the task as well or, worse yet, will fail and it will reflect on you.

I encourage you to shift your assumption from one of *I must do it all for it to be perfect*. Step back and consider this: a person may not do the task exactly like you would do it, but what is the end goal? I used to tell my team, "I want you to understand the end goal. How you get there, I don't care, as long as there is no broken glass along the way. All I care about is that you have effectively achieved the desired results." And that is really our role as a leader—to look at the end results you are trying to achieve.

> Step back and consider this: a person may not do the task exactly like you would do it, but what is the end goal?

What is the price you pay for not letting go? The price of not letting go has an upward effect with senior management and a downward effect with your team. Senior management may view you as being too much in the weeds. That is what my client, Kathleen, was told. The senior management team was looking for her to have more of a strategic versus tactical perspective on the many issues facing the organization. This ultimately hurt her advancement.

Another impact of not letting go can directly affect your team. Some of them may have the ability to rise up and be high performers, but your lack of delegating and micromanaging may hamper their growth.

How do you decide what to delegate? Think about a couple of things. First, where do you as a leader add the greatest value to your team? In what areas do you need to provide your expertise to help them develop the skills they need?

Then ask yourself what areas you tend to add the least value, but you still like to be involved. From those areas, choose some tasks to delegate to the right person for the task.

Delegation is a critical part of a leader's ability to lead. Delegating is a skill that requires practice. You empower the people who work with you by delegating. You stifle their growth by controlling them. To be a more effective leader, you need to delegate tasks, develop your team's ability to perform the tasks, and let go of the less strategic tasks of your work.

Delegation gives you back more time. It frees you to focus on more strategic issues and your team develops new skills. You cannot do these things well if you are micromanaging, controlling every little detail and "in the weeds."

The Leader as a Coach

When coaching first came on the scene, it was viewed as a remedial intervention for executives and managers who had performance problems and needed to be "fixed." Most people back then were seen as successful in their careers because they were experts in a technical, functional, or professional area. You had all the answers. It was a command-and-control type of leadership where the leader was responsible for directing the team. If you were that subject matter expert, you could advance to the next level and eventually become a leader within the organization.

But today, rapid, constant, and disruptive changes are the norm. And no leader has all the answers. In fact, an effective leader-as-coach asks questions instead of providing answers, provides support to their team versus judging them, and facilitates their development to be creative and imaginative versus telling them what has to be done.

Today, leadership and executive coaching are thought of as a strategic investment in the talent within the organization. Many view it as a perk for high-potential candidates. Sir John Whitmore, a leading figure in this field, defined skilled coaching as, "unlocking people's potential to maximize their own performance." He further goes on to say that "Coaching focuses on future possibilities, not past mistakes."[1]

Whitmore introduced the GROW Model to help guide leaders as they coach their team members. GROW is an acronym for Goal, Reality, Options, and Will. In a nutshell, the coach asks the following questions of his or her coachee during each coaching session:

Goal: What do you want at the end of this coaching conversation?

Reality: What is the current situation? What's working? What's not working? What are the key things we need to know about this topic before leaping to a conclusion?

Options: What are your potential options and strategies to move closer to your goal?

Will: What specific actions will you take to progress towards your goal? What resources will you need? How will you hold yourself accountable? What help do you need from me?[2]

Research has shown some of the benefits that organizations derive from coaching include empowering individuals, improving performance, creating high employee commitment, and fostering a deeper level of learning. Emerging leaders receive learning and growth opportunities, and experienced leaders receive satisfaction from guiding and coaching others to achieve their potential. So, coaching benefits not only the organization but the leaders, as well.

Not all conversations lend themselves well to coaching. To recognize when an employee is open to having a coaching conversation, listen to their words. If they use phrases like:

- Do you have time for me to run something by you?

- I'd like to get your point of view about X. Do you have time to discuss it?

- Before I share this with the CEO, I'd love your perspective…

- I need some help.

- Can you give me a reality check?

When you have identified a team member who would be a good candidate for coaching, there are several different types of coaching conversations that you can have. Some topics include:

- Setting goals

- Exploring their career path

- Checking progress on a task, project, or initiative

- Creating a plan

- Motivations and value

- Working through conflict

- Habits that may be holding them back

- Closing skill gaps and improving skills

Asking powerful questions is a cornerstone of effective coaching. In coaching, we believe that the coachee has the answers inside of them, they just don't know it yet. But through the use of powerful questions and sharing experiences, you give them the space to reflect and respond effectively. Use open-ended questions. These types of questions lead them on the road to self-discovery and also lead to honest answers. Adopting a coaching style of leadership is all about communicating more and better. Communicating leads to a higher level of motivation, empowerment, delegation, and trust.

CHAPTER EIGHT

Inclusive Leadership

If you want to go fast, go alone;
if you want to go far, go together.
—African Proverb

Diversity and a lack of inclusion are two reasons I decided to write this book. Diversity often refers to the visible differences we see at first glance: gender, age, race, or physical disability, for example. But there are many differences that cannot be seen: personality, culture, experiences, beliefs, invisible disabilities, sexual orientation, identity, and ethnicity. Ultimately, to embrace diversity is to embrace all the ways that someone is unique—the diversity that is seen, not seen, said, and unsaid.

I was often the only woman and the only person of color in Corporate America. As I watched my White peers soar in the organization with mentors and sponsors receiving feedback to advance them, I couldn't help but wonder, "Where could I have gone with that support?" It has been over half a century since the Civil Rights Act (1964) passed, and there are still workplace environments where a woman of color is the only woman and the only person of color.

Research shows that diversity is a strength for groups because it drives innovation and creativity, which provides a competitive advantage for companies. If you ask a company, "Does creativity matter to you?" they would say, *Absolutely!*

Diversity fuels creativity. Biases in the workplace are impacting creativity. We see evidence of bias in hiring and promotions. I spent my career in the technology industry. If you look at the technology industry today, the demographics are still bleak for non-White professionals.

In 2016, Google reported that its technical workplace was 3% Hispanic, 2% African American, with only 18% of all technical roles held by women. These numbers don't reflect the population at large.

It can be exhausting to know you have what it takes to do the job but to constantly miss out on opportunities. This happens far too often.

Inclusive leadership is critical to help your organization become a more diverse, equitable, and inclusive workplace. With their words and actions, leaders influence company culture and set the tone for embracing diversity and inclusivity in the workplace.

What can you as a leader do to create an inclusive culture? You have to do the work. When I say this, I mean we all have our own biases. When you do the work, you will discover your own. This will help you to be more thoughtful about your decisions and how those decisions affect people. Communicate your commitment to diversity to your team and make sure they understand this is something that is important to you and to the organization. Communicate all of the benefits of having a diverse and inclusive culture. Tell them if they notice you are not walking the talk, to call you on it, and it will be penalty-free and non-judgmental because we are all learning.

To accelerate diversity and inclusion in the workplace, it's important to first understand your people. What are their experiences in the workplace? Do the employees feel included, valued, and able to be their authentic selves? How are leaders already cultivating an inclusive environment?

If you have employee resource groups (ERGs) in your organization, consider supporting the work of the groups by encouraging your employees to get involved and attend events for their own learning. If you are a senior leader, consider becoming an executive sponsor for an ERG group. You can support the groups by mentoring, coaching, advising, and lending your social and organizational capital to the group. One fun thing to do is to get involved in reverse mentoring with one of the rising stars in the group. This sends the message that you are a part of the group and want to learn, as well. And, if your company does not have ERGs, start them. This demonstrates your leadership and commitment to inclusion.

As the leader, it is important to lead the team in continuing to educate everyone. Everyone has the power to make a difference in the workplace, in our community, and in our society. Inclusion is making sure everyone is invited and engaged, regardless of our differences, because together we create value—which translates into the company's competitive advantage.

> Inclusion is making sure everyone is invited and engaged, regardless of our differences, because together we create value—which translates into the company's competitive advantage.

Leading Across Cultures

In the late 90s, when I took on a global leadership role, IBM reached out and suggested that I attend a workshop called, "Managing across Cultures." It really opened my eyes to gaining a better understanding of different cultures. For example, I learned that in a professional environment in Japan, the protocol is for all employees to acknowledge each other based on their last names.

One of my peers, Christine, worked for several years in Japan. She was addressed by her last name followed by the word, "San." She was Cain-San, and she learned quickly that she had to address her colleagues the same way. Also, in Japanese culture, showing respect to your superiors because of their position in the hierarchy is required. You wait until you are asked to provide feedback.

So, what can you do as a leader of a multicultural team? First, encourage open communication, inviting your team members to share their thoughts and ideas openly, and creating a safe space where everyone feels comfortable expressing themselves. Active listening and responding to your team members' feedback is crucial in building trust and understanding.

Take the time to learn about the cultural backgrounds of your team members, their values, beliefs, and customs. By understanding and appreciating cultural differences, you can better understand your team members' perspectives and build stronger connections.

Celebrate the different cultures represented on your team by organizing cultural events or activities. This can help team members learn about each other's cultures and build stronger connections.

By fostering connection within your multicultural team, you can create a positive work environment that encourages collaboration, mutual respect, and innovation.

The business world needs leaders who have a true understanding of and commitment to cultural humility. This will naturally lead to an increased sense of belonging, better communication, higher employee well-being and mental health, better collaboration, and teamwork, and reduced interpersonal conflict. Having a multicultural team is a competitive advantage because you are able to access diverse talent, knowledge, and experiences for your overall solutions.

Leading across Generations

The value a multi-generational team brings to the organization includes innovative results through a diversity of minds, and a rich pool of skill sets. Embracing those differences allows a leader to leverage the differences and achieve competitive and innovative business results.

Effectively leading across generations has a lot to do with understanding what matters to each generation because what matters to them motivates them. An organization that has employees from different generations has the potential to be powerful and innovative. However, melding the different beliefs together can potentially bring conflict.

Understanding what matters to each generation and how they operate is beneficial when leading across generations. The more you know about them, the more you can motivate them. However, don't assume that just because you are in a particular generation the same things matter. Remember each person is an individual and should be treated as such.

The generation we call "Boomers" (born 1946-1964) are generally motivated by upward mobility and often have a single-minded focus. They select a specific goal or objective they want to achieve, and devote all of their energy towards attaining that outcome. Additionally, Boomers tend to prefer face-to-face communication when interacting with others.

Members of Generation X (born 1965-1980) are motivated by career opportunities and are also seeking balance in their lives. They place great importance on aligning their personal values with those of their employer. Growing up during a time when their parents experienced layoffs and divorce was common has made them option-thinkers who value having choices. As such, they appreciate being rewarded for their contributions and are not afraid to challenge the status quo. Finally, they do not believe that the right to lead should be based solely on time invested in the organization, but rather on the value one brings and their overall contributions.

Millennials (born 1981-1995) place great importance on being able to express their ideas and having their input taken seriously. They typically show respect for authority figures and are eager to develop their professional careers while making a positive impact on others and the organization. Meaningful work is essential for them, and they often prefer to act on tasks immediately instead of engaging in long-term planning.

Growing up with technology, they value understanding the business case and the return on investment of their decisions. They seek out companies that offer specific training and development opportunities, along with coaches and mentors.

To motivate Millennials, leaders should communicate how their work matters to the team and the company, including the potential impact of their projects. Getting to know them and providing opportunities that show they are valued members of the team is also crucial. Allowing them to express their opinions is a way to show that their perspectives matter. Constructive feedback is important, and clear communication of expectations regarding goals, timelines, and objectives can help them stay focused and engaged.

Finally, Gen Z (mid-90s to mid-2000s) has begun to enter the workplace. They highly value having a voice, transparency, purpose, and authenticity, and require a clear understanding of the purpose behind tasks to stay motivated. Unlike Boomers, Gen Z believes in integrating work and life, and are skilled in using technology due to growing up with it. They are comfortable with crowdsourcing and experimentation, and view failure as an opportunity to learn and improve. Gen Z works well in small teams with strong leaders, but may need help with interpersonal skills due to spending much of their time on social media and technology products. They seek opportunities for growth and meaningful contributions, and appreciate recognition and rewards that align with their interests.

When managing across generations, focus on the metrics and not the person. Provide clear performance metrics so they know what they are being held accountable to do. When in doubt about how to best motivate a team member, just ask. I did this with one of my direct reports whom I wanted to recognize in a meaningful way. I assumed that she would appreciate monetary recognition, but when I asked her, she said that she preferred a day of paid leave because she had two young children, and it would give her a day to rest.

Consider mentoring with multigenerational teams. Have the more senior team members mentor the junior team members. And use reverse mentoring by having the junior team members mentor the more senior members in technology.

Understanding each generation's approach to learning and when possible, tailoring your management approach can help to create a happy and productive team, making it even more possible to achieve the organization's goals.

Effectively Leading in a Remote/Hybrid Work Environment

Gone are the days when all employees worked under the same roof. Back in the early 2000s, IBM decided to reduce their real estate expenses by moving employees to work from their home offices. Most of my team began working from home, as did I, going into the office two days a week. At the time, my son was in elementary school, so I welcomed the idea of having him come home after school versus going to after-school care. I was thrilled to not have to sit in traffic for an hour just to drive 15 miles to work.

However, once I began working from my home office, I started doing all of my home chores during the day (cooking, laundry, etc.). As a result, I found myself working into the night to finish my tasks. In addition, I had global responsibility. And I had the added pressure of feeling that I had to be available to respond 24/7. There were times when my team members in the U.S. would have to work at night to accommodate those team members that were based in Europe and Asia. That often interfered with my mommy duties like dinner, helping with homework, and bedtime.

Keep in mind there are a lot of reasons to work remote/hybrid. Some of the benefits include more flexibility, better work/life integration, less money spent on work clothes, and less money spent on gas or public transit to get to the office.

But, at the same time, there are some workers who face the emotional effects of loneliness, isolation, and the need to connect in person with their co-workers. So, they want to return to the physical workplace but not necessarily on a full-time basis. This is why there are situations when remote work is appropriate, when hybrid work is appropriate, and when coming into the office each day is appropriate. It depends on the individual. But, as a leader, understand the needs of your people and assess their skill level and whether a remote, hybrid, or office location is best on an individual level.

As a leader, it is important to let your people know that you care by listening to their concerns. Demonstrate empathy, show curiosity, and listen. Have frequent and intentional checkpoints with your people. Ask: How are they doing? How's your family? What challenges are they facing by working from home? How can you best support them? These are all opportunities to build trust.

Here's what I learned: managing remote and hybrid teams requires the same competencies as managing teams who are located physically in the same space; however, there are some skills that are necessary for effective leadership in a remote/hybrid work environment. These are: giving productive coaching/feedback, fostering an inclusive environment, interpersonal skills, and leveraging communication technology to enable collaboration and connection.

Guidelines are important regardless of whether the team is centrally located or remote. Remote teams need clear boundaries within which to operate and make decisions.

Here are a few things to consider:

- Take the time to get to know the challenges and issues remote employees are having. Remember, it is not important that the team members work 9-5 unless they have a job that requires them to be on the phone, like a call center rep. The quality of the product is what is important. Did they complete the tasks in a professional manner and met/exceeded the deadline? Some people work best early in the morning and some people may work best at night. For baby boomers, the norm was to work in the office. In sales, there was this belief that if you were there before your boss came in and stayed until after they left, the manager felt you were working hard. I am so glad that belief flew out the window. It's not about the hours you are working; it is about the results.

- Make sure the team knows your expectations and is clear about what is expected of them. Develop guidelines for how the team *communicates*. Encourage their input and contribution. Recognize and thank them for contributing during the meeting. If someone is not contributing, get them involved by asking for their opinion/feedback. Create standards for email, document sharing, and tools for one-on-one conversations. Let the purpose of the meeting determine the best method of communicating.

Discuss with your team to think twice before sending emails because the way things are communicated through email can come across very differently than intended. There are some things that are best communicated the old fashion way—by picking up the phone. When sending emails, I make it a practice to ask for acknowledgement of receipt of the email, so I know that it has been received. Encourage the same from the team. If there is a deadline that their response is needed, be sure to include it in the correspondence.

- Determine *meeting agendas*, procedures, and follow-up. Who really needs to be in that meeting? Limit the invitees to only those people that need to be in the meeting. Prior to each meeting, send your agenda out so everyone knows what will be covered and what is expected of them. The agenda should include the time of the meeting, the meeting objectives, the speakers/presenters, the invitee list, and discussion items. I always include times next to each item on the agenda. This helps to keep you on track, so the meeting does not run over. Ask if there are any additional items that should be added to the agenda.

- Set and maintain clear performance standards. Ensure team goals are clear to everyone and that the team works together on problem-solving and brainstorming.

- If the meeting is a virtual meeting, record it for anyone who wants to replay it or for anyone that isn't available to attend. Send out a summary of the meeting with key action items, responsible individuals, and due dates.

This ensures that everyone knows what they are responsible for.

• Working at home can make some people feel isolated. Keep a pulse on each team member. Check in periodically just to find out how they are doing. Prior to each meeting, consider adding an additional 15 minutes on the front end for anyone that wants to pop in and just connect.

• Wrap up and close the meeting by checking for these things:
  ° **Are we complete?** Does anyone have anything else to say or ask?
  ° **Are we aligned?** Is everyone okay with where we ended the discussion?
  ° **What are the next steps?** Are we clear on the actions and deadlines?

All of these skills build upon each other to ensure you have what it takes to be a leader to a diverse and inclusive group of people in various aspects of the job. By working to develop and hone your skills in each of these areas, you can elevate your success—because as a leader, your success depends on your team's performance. Leaders matter more today than ever! By doing these things, you build an inclusive, high-performance workplace for all employees.

Now that you have the knowledge to expertly *lead your team*, in the next chapter we'll focus on the competencies you need as a leader to be an asset to your *organization*.

KEY TAKEAWAYS

1. Adopting a leadership mindset that what you don't know, you can find the resources to figure out will serve you well as a leader.

2. Getting started in a "new" leadership role requires that you understand the business objectives, uncover the challenges, and develop key relationships.

3. Developing your people gives them an opportunity to gain experience and to take on new jobs and responsibilities to set them up to be more competitive.

4. The success of an organization depends on how well its leaders collaborate. Always make your direct reports, as well as other members of the organization, feel welcome. Walk the floor so they know that you are there to help with any issues.

5. Mastering delegation, performance management, coaching, and emotional intelligence are four skills to quickly help you to be more impactful and effective as a leader.

6. Diversity and Inclusion is a strength for groups because it fosters more innovation when you have a team that has gender, racial, and cultural diversity and when the individual members feel that they belong on the team.

7. Remote and hybrid environments aren't going away. Effective leaders understand the pros and cons of working from home, and create thoughtful ways to keep team members involved and engaged efficiently.

IT'S ABOUT THE ORGANIZATION

There is one quality which one must possess to win,
and that is definiteness of purpose, the knowledge of
what one wants, and a burning desire to possess it.
—Napoleon Hill

When I joined IBM, I worked as a Technical Sales rep in the Sales Division. The Sales Division's primary focus was—unsurprisingly—on making our revenue targets, commonly referred to as sales quotas. At the beginning of each year, the leadership team determined our revenue targets. Based on that target, each sales rep determined what hardware, software, and services we would have to sell to achieve our revenue targets. Our compensation was based on making or exceeding these targets.

So, it's a funny thing—when you are paid based on what you install, you pay attention to what is being sold. You want to make sure it's the right product for your client, or otherwise, they'll return it, and you lose your commission. With training, I became very good at working with clients to manage the installation of their software products. But it wasn't long before I realized I needed to understand the business more comprehensively.

I can't begin to tell you the number of times I sat at the lunch table or went out for drinks after work with my White male colleagues, and the conversation was about the current events in the news and the impact they had on IBM's stock. They talked about the stock analysts' reports, the earnings reports, IBM's quarterly report, and which stocks they purchased. They checked their stocks every day.

Being a first-generation corporate hire, all of this was new and foreign to me, so I decided to go back to school to get my MBA. That was one of the best decisions I made in my life because I gained an understanding of how business works.

Business acumen and ethics are at the top of the competencies that a good leader needs to develop. People with strong business acumen understand the big picture and the core functions of business and industry. They understand business issues and are able to adapt and remain agile during times of change. They know the operations of the business and are insightful about how to achieve goals and ensure business success.

Business acumen spans the entire company. As a leader, you need to focus on your organization and how you can impact it. Being able to speak the language of strategy and finance builds credibility. Strengthening your business acumen, understanding your role, its function within the organization, and the ways in which your role could be developed are key factors in your career progression.

Business acumen competency includes three major areas:

- *Strategic Acumen:* Understanding the strategic perspective of the business or its business strategies. It's how the business makes money. I often refer to this as comprehending the big picture–where the business is today, where the business needs to go, and how to get there. This knowledge is critical to becoming an influential leader.

- *Financial Acumen:* Understanding the story that the numbers tell and taking appropriate action, strategic and/or tactical, based on those numbers. You must recognize what drives growth, profitability, and cash flow, the company's financial statements, and key performance measures.

- *Business Agility:* Understanding how a business can thrive and stay competitive in the digital age. It means being able to swiftly adapt to market changes and seize emerging opportunities by implementing innovative business solutions. To meet the ever-increasing speed of the market and deliver exceptional customer satisfaction, it is crucial to validate innovations with customers and be ready to pivot when circumstances change.

These are all components that will help you make better business decisions. As Jeff McCreary, former Chief Sales and Marketing Officer for Texas Instruments said, "If your organization doesn't fully understand how your company thrives economically and how it delivers distinct value to the marketplace, you won't be as successful as you can and should be."[1]

Throughout this section, I will review these three major competencies in business acumen. You may feel that this doesn't apply to you, or you may feel uncomfortable reading it because of the new concepts. But if you want to advance in your career, you will have to master these competencies to be valued as a leader in the organization. While I acknowledge it may feel like a little bit of a "dry" read, I encourage you not to skip this section and to come back to it as needed.

CHAPTER NINE

Think and Act Strategically

Strategic thinking helps to bridge between
where you are and where you want to be.
—Pearl Zhu

Business acumen is the ability to discern the strategic perspective of the business. When you develop this competency, you are often viewed as a strategic thinker. Strategic thinking involves seeing the big picture of your business and the specific paths to its growth amid changing consumer trends and competition.

Having business acumen means understanding all the ways your business makes money and knowing how to put the measurements in place that increase profitability. As an executive, your strategic thinking skills and business acumen competency are fundamental in shaping powerful strategies for organizational growth. Being a strategic thinker is a skill needed to grow and move into higher levels of leadership.

I remember sitting in my own first strategic planning session; my manager thought it would be a great experience for me to attend. I sat there impressed, listening to the thought leaders discuss industry standards and what our competitors were doing in the marketplace. But because of my limited understanding of strategy, I contributed very little during the meeting. I decided that day I would be better prepared the next time.

What is Strategy?

Strategy is a way of describing how you are going to get things done. It is less specific than an action plan (which tells the who-what-when). Instead, a strategy broadly answers two questions, *Where do you want to go?* and *How do we get there from here?* It looks at a situation and figures out how to differentiate the organization from its competitors, considering existing barriers and resources (people, money, materials, power, etc.), as well as the overall mission, vision, and objectives of the initiative. In other words, a strategy helps determine how to realize the vision and objectives of the initiative.

A strategic thinker is always planning for the future, anticipating obstacles, and preparing for both adverse and positive outcomes. He or she provides future-oriented, creative solutions to problems. This is a skill that will distinguish you from others and help you contribute value to the organization.

Strategic thinking skills are among the most highly sought-after leadership competencies. Leaders capable of thinking logically, critically, and strategically can set themselves apart from their peers and have a major impact on their business's trajectory. Strategic thinking skills enable you to solve complex problems and address challenges to achieve business objectives.

> Leaders capable of thinking logically,
> critically, and strategically can set themselves
> apart from their peers and have a major
> impact on their business's trajectory.

A *Harvard Business Review* article lists six essential skills that are needed to be able to think strategically.[2] These skills include the ability to anticipate, challenge, interpret, decide, align, and learn. Effective and adaptive leaders apply all six of these skills at once.

- *Anticipate.* To improve your ability to anticipate, you must constantly talk to your customers, suppliers, and partners to understand their challenges. Research and look for ways to solve their challenges. Keep your eye on industry trends. Understand what the best in the industry are doing, and *set* industry trends versus *following* industry trends. Conduct market research to understand what your competitors are doing.

- *Challenge.* Strategic thinkers must be willing to challenge the status quo and encourage different points of view. One of my coaching clients felt that if anyone did not agree with him, they were not part of his team. Through coaching, I helped him understand that different opinions would increase his options and possibly generate more solutions.

  In challenging the status quo, focus on the root cause of the problem versus the symptoms. List your assumptions and allow brainstorming. It is also good to get input from others who do not have an ulterior motive. Ask questions like:

- ○ What are we doing today?
- ○ Why are we doing this work? Why now?
- ○ Does this work matter?
- ○ How can we position ourselves to enter a new market?
- ○ How should we respond to this threat from our competitors?
- ○ What's our direction for growth for these products and services?
- ○ What does success look like for our team?
- ○ What else can we do to achieve more, better, faster?

- *Decide.* There will be times when you will have to make difficult decisions with incomplete information and must do so quickly. Strategic thinkers look at multiple options and don't lock themselves into only one way. They know that it's important to have a disciplined process for making those quick decisions. They look at the trade-offs involved, pros and cons, as well as both the short- and long-term goals. Then, they must have the courage to act.

You may not get it right 100% of the time, but with a disciplined approach, you greatly increase your odds of getting it right most of the time. To improve your ability to decide, always ask, "What other options do we have?" Determine who should be involved and who can influence the success of the decision. Communicate where you are in the process directly with those who should know. And, in many cases, rather than jump directly into implementing the full decision, start with a pilot and see how it goes.

- *Align.* Strategic leaders must be able to find common ground and get the buy-in of their stakeholders, who often have different agendas. Communicating, building trust, and frequently engaging the stakeholders are needed if the strategic leader is to be successful in their role. Always seek to find out how the work aligns with the bigger picture. Are there gaps not being addressed?

  To improve your ability to align, communicate early and often. You don't want a key stakeholder to say, "No one asked me." Identify key stakeholders and the role they play relative to your initiative. Look for hidden agendas. Reach out to understand any concerns and address them. Recognize those colleagues who support team alignment.

- *Interpret.* Getting feedback from various sources provides an opportunity to look at different perspectives. Synthesize all the input and analyze it. This process will allow you to recognize patterns and seek new insights for other ways to solve the problem. To improve your ability to interpret, look for at least three possible explanations for what you're observing. Invite different perspectives. Zoom in on the details and then out to see the big picture. Look for missing information and draw your hypothesis. Question the assumptions and play devil's advocate. Then step away from the problem.

Do something different, like going to the gym, listening to music, or going for a walk. Then, come back to the problem. You may see it from a totally different light.

• *Learn.* Strategic leaders promote a culture of being curious. Because they know people learn from failures, they are not afraid to fail. My branch manager encouraged leaders to publish stories about failures that ultimately led to creative solutions. I recall we had an innovative tournament one year to see who could generate the most creative ideas across the organization. This generated many great ideas we wouldn't have had if we didn't step outside the box and try something new. To improve your ability to learn, document lessons learned, reward leaders who try something but fail in terms of outcomes, identify processes or initiatives that are not producing as expected, and examine their root causes. Send the message that a creative culture is valued, and mistakes are nothing more than learning opportunities.

A Valuable Tool

A strategic plan is a valuable tool to help leaders and the organization to achieve market outcomes. It enables you to track progress toward your goals. When each department and team understands the company's larger strategy, their progress can directly impact the success of the organization. Yet, according to a survey by Bridges Business Consultancy, only 68% of professionals believe their organization is good at developing strategy.[3]

Other reasons to employ a strategic plan include:

• Planning medium- to long-term strategies for a project or for the business.

- Making better decisions about what to do in day-to-day operations because the leader understands the overarching vision, mission, and goals of the organization. This top-down approach can be tracked by using Objectives and Key Results (OKRs) and Key Performance Indicators (KPIs).

- Setting direction and priorities to create a forward-focused vision that can align with your organization and its shareholders and allows the organization to adjust its direction in response to a changing environment.

- Simplifying decision-making by making decisions based on the organization's vision and mission.

- Communicating the company's goals–how and why those goals were chosen and what they can do to help reach those goals–creates a sense of responsibility throughout the organization.

Every organization is different; however, there are some common primary components of a basic strategic planning meeting.

Someone must determine the key players and stakeholders for the project or initiative and then invite them to come together and craft the strategic plan. A strategy manager will measure and monitor the progress of the strategy and report progress to the team and appropriate leaders.

The primary components of a strategic planning meeting include:

- Vision statement
- Mission statement

- Core values (also known as the guiding principles)
- Goals
  - ◦ For each goal, list objectives.
  - ◦ For each objective, define the critical success factors (CSFs), barriers, and strategies.
  - ◦ For each strategy, list the action items that need to be implemented

Strategic Planning Process

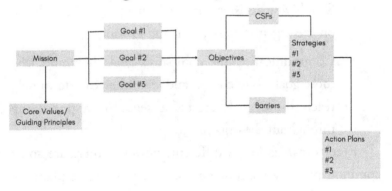

Vision

The ability to envision the future, communicate that vision, and have others buy in is incredibly important for leaders to develop. Being forward-looking and having the ability to envision a future and inspire others to share that vision differentiates leaders.

The vision statement is all about what the company wants to achieve. As a leader, this should be part of your DNA as you look for opportunities for the company to thrive. Some people may refer to vision as the purpose of the organization or the initiative.

The objective of both is to clarify *why* the organization, the project, or the initiative exists.

In addition to fully understanding a company's overarching vision, leaders also must create a vision for any new projects or initiatives and communicate it well. Your team needs to be on the same page. They need to feel that they are a part of this vision. Only then will you get agreement and commitment.

Communicating vision includes three elements:

1. *Clarity* – Tell the team where the initiative/project needs to go and what needs to be accomplished.

2. *Strategy* – Share ideas for how this might be accomplished, but more importantly, solicit input from the team.

3. *Gratitude* – Communicate how much you appreciate the value your team adds to achieving the vision.

Once you've communicated these three things, get out of the way, and let your team make it happen.

Mission

When you know what you want to achieve (vision), you need to define how you will achieve the vision. The mission statement is your road map for getting there, or how you plan to accomplish the vision. It should be clear and concise. It lays out your organizational, project, or initiative goals and how to achieve them.

The mission statement is the guiding light that inspires you to help others in the organization understand how they can contribute to your company's high performance.

Let's look at some mission statements of other companies:

- Google: *To organize the world's information and make it universally accessible and useful.*

- Apple: *To bring the best personal computing products and support to students, educators, designers, scientists, engineers, businesspersons, and consumers in over 140 countries around the world.*

- Netflix: *To entertain the world.*

Core Values/Guiding Principles

A company's core values are the guiding principles for how a company behaves. Everyone should be aligned around these guiding principles to serve employees, customers, and the broader community.

In many ways, *values* and *culture* are synonymous. They're both about the higher aspirations of a company. The result is that a company's culture is its DNA, which is fundamental to a company's identity.

People join companies for many reasons. I joined IBM because of its company culture and because it had one of the best training companies in the Fortune 500 companies. I felt that it was a good fit for me because my values aligned with the organization's values.

Although occasionally bureaucracy made it difficult for our sales teams to be agile enough to meet the customer's needs, IBM allowed its people to be creative and innovative. IBM reinvented itself year after year through technology. New products were developed, resulting in the company being a leader in its industry.

After some bumpy years preceding the 21st century, IBM brought in new leadership, headed by Louis V. (Lou) Gerstner, Jr., and Lou engaged employees by asking for their feedback relative to core values. He asked questions like, "What values do you think should guide us as a company?" What we ended up with in 2003 for a core values statement was, in many ways, a modern restatement of the original core values of IBM in 1914 with which the company had experienced such success:

1914 Core Values	2003 Core Values
Respect for the individual, superlative customer service, and the pursuit of excellence in all tasks.	Dedication to every client's success. Innovation that matters, for our company and for the world. Trust and personal responsibility in all relationships.

Lou later said, "I came to see, in my time at IBM, that culture isn't just one aspect of the game—it *is* the game. In the end, an organization is nothing more than the collective capacity of its people to create value."[4]

Setting Goals

After the vision, mission, and core values are set, it's time to develop goals. A goal is a general statement of what you want to achieve—a milestone that you want to achieve in the process of implementing a strategy.

Goals should be simple and easy to understand. For each goal, think about what success looks like if accomplished; then identify actionable tasks to achieve the goal. Does the goal align with the values of the organization? Is the goal attainable? Is the goal adaptable, and can it be changed, as needed?

Actions are tactical tasks that need to be done to achieve the goal. For example:

Measurable Goal	Action Strategy
Increase sales by 20% in 12 months.	Marketing department will create and implement a plan to increase sales in regions 2 and 6.
Identify and retain industry consultants by March 31.	Create a team to talk to the marketing, sales, and finance organizations to get a list of their top 5 consultants. Select a small group to interview. Hire 4 industry consultants.

Metrics to Evaluate Strategic Plan

There is an old saying that "what you measure gets attention." If sales are measured and increase, you will know it, and you can reward the sales team. Performance measurements are key to effective business performance. Creating a dashboard of Key Performance Indicators (KPI) results is an easy way to communicate results to your organization, stakeholders, and leaders.

KPIs are measurable values that demonstrate how effective a company is relative to achieving its key business objectives. They help drive growth, spot problem areas, and identify potential areas for improvement. KPIs are only as valuable as the actions they inspire and should originate with data that comes from the strategic planning session. Together, all of these elements are needed to create strong KPIs that will drive the results forward:

- What is your desired outcome?

- How will it be measured?
- How will you know when you have achieved this outcome?
- How often do you review progress against your outcome?

CHAPTER TEN

Financial Acumen

*Financial literacy is just as important
in life as the other basics.*
—John W. Rogers Jr.

Financial acumen is understanding what drives growth, profitability, and cash flow. It helps you to better manage your resources, assess risks, implement new technologies, and improve the level of customer satisfaction. It's crucial to know the financial aspect so you can determine the health of the company and how your actions are impacting the bottom line.

Depending on your position in the business, you may not need to understand the financial numbers as well as a leader does, but financial knowledge will only help you to realize the monetary impact of your decisions. If you don't possess financial acumen, it will be extremely difficult to run the business or contribute properly as a leader.

To know the financial status of the company, there are three core financial statements you need to understand—Income Statement, Cash Flow Statement, and Balance Sheet. In this chapter, we will briefly discuss the purpose of each statement. To gain a broader understanding of these financial tools, look for the appropriate training.

Income Statement:

The Income Statement (often called the Profit & Loss Statement, or P&L) is crucial to a company's survival. It shows whether an organization has made or lost money over a given period of time. In other words, it shows if your business is profitable. It tells you whether your revenue is higher than your expenses, and whether you are actually making a profit.

In "It's About You," we discussed the fact that understanding and managing P&L can be a major contributor to helping you make a career move. When you are running your business and far exceeding the profit targets, people within the organization will listen to you. This is one way to prove your value to the organization.

As a leader within my own global organization, I continuously monitored my P&L. I could quickly tell how the team was performing relative to profit and make decisions based on my "bottom line."

A P&L Statement can help you answer questions about your overall business strategy, the day-to-day operations, and company trends:[5]

Overall business strategy:

- Does your revenue cover your costs and expenses?
- What's the return on investment (ROI) for your business expenses?

- Is there enough money from the proceeds to cover your pay?

Day-to-day operations:

- Which products/services are your high- and low-earning revenue streams?

- Which categories are your greatest expenses?

- What is your gross margin to revenue?

- Which expenses can you lower?

Company trends:

- Factors impacting the company's profitability and revenue growth

- How the business is progressing financially over a specified period of time

- The company's sales patterns compared to the industry trends

The P&L Statement includes five main sections:

- **Income/revenue:** The total amount of money received from sales of goods/services

- **COGS:** Cost of materials and time involved in producing the goods/service

- **Expenses:** Costs associated with operating your business—what you're paying other people and businesses, including payroll, utilities, hardware, software, and travel

- **Other income/expenses:** Irregular transactions not associated with daily operations

- **Net income**: The difference between your income and expenses, which shows if your business is making a profit or a loss

Cash Flow Statement:

A company's P&L may reflect a profit, but that does not mean it has enough money to pay for expenses like wages and materials. To determine that, leaders must look at the Cash Flow Statement, which, just like the name says, shows the cash coming into and going out of the business. In other words, the P&L shows a bigger picture, while the Cash Flow Statement is a breakdown focusing on the flow of cash through the business.

With a complete picture of how well the company is prepared to pay expenses and where in the business that money might be held, this statement is used by leaders to ensure the business is solvent, by investors to monitor their investment, and by financial professionals to determine if the company can pay its creditors.

Balance Sheet:

The Balance Sheet shows the overview of the company's financial position and reflects what the company owes and owns during a specified period of time by evaluating liabilities and equity.

A Balance Sheet is divided into Assets, Liabilities, and Shareholder's Equity.

- Assets: the sum of cash on hand, short-term obligations that your customers owe you (known as accounts receivable), inventory, and your long-term operating assets, such as land & buildings, plant & equipment, and furniture and fixtures.

- Liabilities: short-term operating expenses such as utility bills, income tax, wages, and accounts payable. Liabilities are derived from Assets less Shareholder's Equity.

- Shareholder's Equity: the amount of money that would most likely be left over if a company liquidated all of its assets to pay off its liabilities. This represents the money that shareholders would receive in exchange for their investment. Equity is derived from Assets less Liabilities.

As the name implies, everything in this statement must balance.

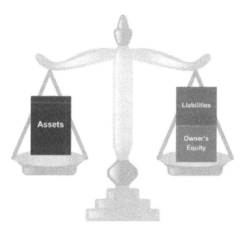

By having a clear understanding of how transactions impact the company's financial position, you will be a better decision-maker.

In summary, P&L, Cash Flow Statement, and Balance Sheet are interlinked. The same financial data is used for each of them; however, each shows a different aspect of the financial health of the company.

- The P&L tells how much profit or loss your company has had over a certain period of time.

- The Cash Flow Statement shows how much cash has moved into and out of the company over a certain period of time.

- The Balance Sheet reflects the financial status of your company for a specific point in time. All assets are balanced against liabilities and owner's equity.

CHAPTER ELEVEN

Business Agility

Innovation is key. Only those who have the agility to change with the market and innovate quickly will survive.
—Robert Kiyosaki

Business Agility is all about understanding how to adapt, change quickly, and be more competitive in a rapidly changing, ambiguous, and turbulent business environment. It includes knowing how to position the company to compete with competitors, and how to stay current relative to global issues and technology changes within the industry.

A business model—a tool that provides information about an organization's target market, the market needs, and the role that their products and services play in meeting those needs—will steer a company down the path to success. Understanding the company's business model will enable you to make better business decisions. In order to position the company to win, it's important to know your customers and what they want, your competitors and what they have to offer, and the industry trends shaping the marketplace.

Organizations today operate in a highly competitive global environment. Now more than ever, innovation is critical to a company's sustained success. This is evident with the once-popular video rental chains like Blockbuster, which closed their stores due to the rise of the online streaming services offered by companies like Netflix and Amazon.

"Companies need to be fast-moving, and their employees and managers need to be comfortable with assessing the global landscape and enabling their organization to change. If they don't do that, companies tend to slowly fade away,"[6] says Tucker Marion, an associate professor at Northeastern University's D'Amore-McKim School of Business and director of the Master of Science in Innovation program. "Innovation is coming up with new services, products, and processes to transform a company either through new sources of revenue, new business models, or new ways to consider how the company operates."[7]

Products and services play a part in meeting those needs. Marion addresses three types of innovation: product innovation, process innovation, and business model innovation.[8]

- **Product Innovation**: The development of a new product, as well as an improvement in the performance or features of an existing product; it's what typically comes to mind when someone says "innovation." Apple's continued iteration of its iPhone is an example of product innovation.

- **Process Innovation**: The implementation of new or improved production and delivery methods in an effort to increase a company's production levels and reduce costs. One of the most notable examples is when Ford Motor Company introduced the first moving assembly line more than a century ago, dropping the assembly time for a single vehicle from twelve hours to roughly ninety minutes.

- **Business Model Innovation**: These are the changes in the business model related to how a product is brought to market. For example, Amazon began serving as a channel for other retailers to market their products, giving them the ability to take a cut of each purchase without needing to maintain inventory of slower-selling products.

Business Model Canvas

The Business Model Canvas is a tool that helps people quickly understand the marketplace model that was developed by Alexander Osterwalder, a Swiss entrepreneur and strategist. Osterwalder said he developed the Business Model Canvas because "lengthy business plans often increase the risk of failure."

The Business Model Canvas (BMC)[9] is the standard used not only by startups, but also by established companies like Microsoft, GE, and Mastercard. The main focus is to establish the foundation of a company's business model in a simple process; however, it also helps in enhancing a company's business as it evolves. The framework is simple and lays out the fundamental elements for a business to make money while delivering its unique value proposition.

The key benefits of using the Business Model Canvas are that it:

- Addresses the most important elements when launching new products and services.

- Helps you envision how to sell your products, the type of resources needed, and the different customer segments to serve, which gives you clarity when talking to customers.

- Assists with the execution steps necessary to take your idea to market. Connecting the dots between your value proposition, customer segments, and revenue streams is a good input to your marketing strategy positioning statement as well as your sales strategy.

The Business Model Canvas:[10]

Key Partners

Who are our key partners?
Who are our key suppliers?
Which key resources are we acquiring from them?

Types of partnership
-Strategic alliance
-Cooperation
-Joint ventures
-Buyer-supplier relationships

Key Activities

What key activities do our value propositions require?
Our distribution channels?
Customer relationships?
Revenue streams?

Categories
-Production
-Problem-solving
-Platform/Network

Key Resources

What key resources do our value propositions require?

Types of resources
-Human
-Physical
-Intellectual
-Financial

Value Propositions

What values do we deliver to the customer?
Which one of our customer's problems are we trying to solve?
What products and services are we offering to our customer segments?
Which customer needs are we satisfying?

Customer Relationships

What type of relationships do our customers expect us to establish and maintain with them? Which ones have we established? How costly are they?
-Personal assistance
-Dedicated personal assistance
-Self-service
-Automated services
-Communities
-Co-creation

Channels

Through which channels do our customers want to be reached? How are we reaching them now? Which ones work best and are cost-efficient?

Types of channels
-Owned channels
-Partner channels

Customer Segments

For whom are we creating value?
Who are our most important customers?

Customer segment types
-Mass market
-Niche market
-Segmented
-Diversified
-Multi-sided platform

Cost Structure

What are the most important costs inherent in our business model? Which key resources and activities are most expensive? Is our business more cost-driven or value-driven?

Revenue Streams

For what value our customers are willing to pay? For what do they currently pay? How are they currently paying? How much does each revenue stream contribute to our overall revenues?

Types of revenue stream
-Asset sales   -Lending/leasing/renting   -Advertising
-Usage fee   -Licensing
-Subscription fee   -Brokerage fees

Example of the Business Model Canvas:[11]

Business Model Canvas - NETFLIX

• Key Partners	• Key Activities	• Value Propositions	• Customer Relationships	• Customer Segments
Internet service providers (ISP) 3rd party studios	Content procurement Application development 3rd party licensing	On-demand video Huge selection of content Original content Competitive price point	Self-service platform	Mass market
	• Key Resources		• Channels	
	Streaming rights Internet bandwidth Recommendation algorithm Content library		Website App store Affiliate partners	

• Cost	• Revenue Streams
In-house content production 3rd party licensing Streaming application (staff, maintenance, etc.)	Subscriptions

Developing business acumen is an ongoing process that requires time, dedication, and attention. To improve your business acumen skills and competencies:[12]

- Join professional or industry associations where there is a wealth of knowledge and the ability to network.

- Read business books, magazines, LinkedIn, and blogs on marketing, leadership, financial skills, and business development.

- Enroll in business training workshops on financial acumen.

- Learn from colleagues.

- Find experts in your business area and learn from their experiences.

- If you work for a publicly owned company, look at their annual reports, focusing on gross profit, net profit, cash on hand, assets, and liabilities.

Whew! Thank you for sticking with me to the end of this section. As you can see, it takes specialized skills to succeed as a leader. Your business acumen, consisting of strategic acumen, financial acumen, and business agility, is the foundation upon which businesses will rise to market dominance or crumble. Strengthening your business acumen will enable you to make better decisions and significantly benefit the company.

> Strengthening your business acumen will enable you to make better decisions and significantly benefit the company.

Now that we have established the foundation of your leadership skills so you can positively impact the organization, it's time to discuss building a community, which, from my perspective, is where the fun begins as you learn to collaborate and build influential relationships to achieve the purpose of the business.

SECTION THREE
KEY TAKEAWAYS

1. Strengthening your business acumen, understanding your role, its function within the organization, and the ways in which your role could be developed are key factors in your career progression.

2. Strategic acumen, the first skill in business acumen, is the ability to discern the strategic perspective of the business. Being a strategic thinker is a skill needed to grow and move into higher levels of leadership.

3. Being forward-looking and having the ability to envision a future and inspire others to share that vision differentiates leaders. Communicating vision includes clarity, strategy, and gratitude.

4. A leader must possess financial acumen and recognize what drives growth, profitability, and cash flow, the company's financial statements, and key performance measures.

5. Leaders also need to have business agility, an understanding of how to adapt, change quickly, and be more competitive in a rapidly changing, ambiguous, turbulent environment.

SECTION FOUR
IT'S ABOUT THE COMMUNITY

Volunteering is at the very core of being a human.
No one has made it through life without
someone else's help.
—Heather French Henry

When I sat down to think about the Rising Leader Model, I knew that Community had to be a part of it. Growing up in the South, my family was actively involved in our community. My father made sure he took church members to register to vote and later to cast their vote at the polls, and he was always visiting the sick and making sure that Vacation Bible School was a part of the annual community events. My mother started the first African American Girl Scouts organization in our community. So, for me, the community was what helped me to grow and develop as a person. It helped me understand the value of giving back. That's why it is my hope that spotlighting the importance of being actively engaged in your community will also help you grow both professionally and personally.

Becoming involved in the local community not only broadens personal leadership skills but also generates favorable public relations for your business or organization. Being known as a positive contributor to the community is a win-win proposition for both you and your company. A business is only as strong as the community of which it is a part.

CHAPTER TWELVE

The Benefits of Giving Back

Life is never made unbearable by circumstances,
but only by lack of meaning and purpose.
—Victor Frankl

Giving back to your community is a key component of becoming your best self, well-balanced in both your professional and personal life. Volunteering allows you to share your expertise with others. It gives you a sense of purpose, widens your network, shares your expertise, and helps you grow as a leader.

More and more studies are showing how our physical and mental health can benefit through volunteering. United Healthcare stated, "The *2017 Doing Good is Good for You Study*, in partnership with VolunteerMatch, confirmed these results: from feeling better to enhancing well-being and providing a sense of personal enrichment and satisfaction (in other words, being happier), 'doing good' is good for you. Let's not forget that people who are happier live longer!"[1]

There are many benefits to volunteering for the individual, the employee, and the company.

Benefits for the Individual

The *2017 Doing Good is Good for You Study* cited these proven positive effects that volunteering has on our physical and mental health:

- 75% of people who volunteered in the past 12 months reported feeling physically healthier.

- 34% of people who volunteered found that participating in these activities helped them better manage their chronic illnesses. Compared with those who had not volunteered in the past 12 months, volunteers were 78% more likely to feel they had control over their health.

- The connection between volunteering and mental/emotional health is even more dramatic–93% noted an improvement in mood, 79% had lower stress levels, and 88% saw an improvement in self-esteem. Volunteers believe they are calmer, more peaceful, and had more energy to a greater extent than those who had not volunteered in the past year.[2]

Of people who volunteered in the past 12 months...

88%
note improved self-esteem

93%
note an improvement in mood

75%
feel physically healthier

78%
feel they have greater control over their health and well-being

79%
experience lower stress levels

34%
can better manage their chronic illnesses

Based on these findings, it's clear that volunteering enhances the lives of the volunteers in a myriad of ways. The same study noted that volunteering "enriches our sense of purpose, emotional well-being, and overall satisfaction with our lives." This healthier, more fulfilled outlook is accompanied by added social benefits, like developing friendships through volunteer activities. Volunteers also report a higher capacity to enjoy socializing compared to those who do not volunteer."[3]

When my son, Michael, was growing up, he loved every sport invented. When he found out we were not going to support him in playing all of them, he finally settled on basketball, tennis, swimming, and football. Working a full-time job while also being his personal chauffeur was challenging for me but really rewarding. I found myself getting even further involved by volunteering to be a team mom, taking the lead with fundraising activities and end-of-the-season team recognition events. Spending time with him and getting to know the boys on his teams as well as their parents was lots of fun.

Volunteering also provides wonderful opportunities for professional development and personal growth. Some ways volunteering can develop your professional skills include:

- **Networking**: Volunteering provides a unique opportunity for individuals to meet new people within their community, including community leaders. Forming key relationships will create new prospects and possibilities for you.

- **Learn new techniques**: Sharpen old skills or build new ones as you perform your volunteer duties. This is an excellent way to experiment with or practice new techniques and skills such as management, customer service, and leadership, which can elevate your current employment and also looks great on a resume. You can even establish your expertise in areas like public speaking, presenting, technology, training, and leadership. The more you practice these skills, the more confident you will be.

- **Serving as a board member:** Serving on a volunteer committee or board is a great way to learn group dynamics and teamwork, and working as a committee chair increases facilitation skills. For example, planning and implementing a major fundraising event can develop goal-setting, planning, and budgeting skills. And supervising and training volunteers can expand your supervisory and training skills.

Through your volunteer work, you might also grow personally by

- Selflessly helping others
- Promoting happiness
- Improving your health
- Building interpersonal skills
- Becoming more culturally aware and learning more about different perspectives
- Realizing everyone has struggles to deal with
- Immersing yourself in the uncomfortable and making an impact
- Feeling satisfaction in knowing you are doing good

- Gaining visibility and exposure to a wide variety of people in the community
- Developing leadership skills
- Finding a sense of belonging
- Achieving balance in your life

Volunteering is a way to put good into the world. When we collaborate and work to support each other, the world becomes a better place, and we gain a sense of fulfillment. It is a great and powerful thing.

Benefits for the Employer

When employees are healthy and perform well, employers reap the benefits. The *2017 Doing Good is Good for You* Study identified three major ways that employers benefit from their employees' volunteering:

- Employees are happier and healthier, resulting in better productivity and reduced sick time.
- Employees develop their professional skills by learning better time management skills (86%), developing their people skills/teamwork (92%), and strengthening relationships (77%).
- Employees are more engaged.[4]

These benefits to employers can greatly affect their bottom line. As a result, employers should encourage their employees to volunteer. By doing so, they can also make a difference in the lives of their employees and the community.

CHAPTER THIRTEEN

Employers are Making a Difference

Business has the power to change lives,
and the best businesses are those that make a positive
difference in their communities.
—Richard Branson

According to the 2021 Gartner's annual survey of CEOs and other senior business executives, environmental sustainability is now a top-ten business focus for the first time in the history of the survey. With growing fears about the state of the environment and the ability to prove ROI for sustainability practices, businesses are under increasing pressure to not only behave ethically and responsibly, but also to demonstrate that they are doing so.[5]

More and more companies want to ensure they operate in a sustainable way and have an impact on society, the organization, and the economy. In order to do so, they are identifying Corporate Social Responsibility goals (CSRs).

As companies shape their CSR strategy, many of them will look at the seventeen key goals for global development the United Nations formally adopted in 2015. These seventeen goals, referred to as Sustainable Development Goals (SDGs), provide a global framework that focuses on a myriad of social needs related to People, Peace, Planet and Prosperity.

The 17 SDGs include:

- No Poverty
- Zero Hunger
- Good Health and Well-Being
- Quality Education
- Gender Equality
- Clean Water and Sanitation
- Affordable and Clean Energy
- Decent Work and Economic Growth
- Industry, Innovation, and Infrastructure
- Reduced Inequalities
- Sustainable Cities and Communities
- Responsible Consumption and Production
- Climate Action
- Life below Water
- Life on Land
- Peace, Justice, and Strong Institutions
- Partnerships for the Goals

Businesses are aligning their CSR strategies to the SDGs. Typically, companies will take responsibility to promote growth in society and focus on their individual enterprise as compared to the global goals of SDGs. They may pick a few of the SDG goals that align with their mission and implement those goals as a part of their CSR.

Kellogg is a good example. Kellogg's *Better Days* is their promise to advance sustainable and equitable access to food by addressing the intersection of wellbeing, hunger, sustainability, and equity, diversion and inclusion. They believe our changing climate is impacting the health of people and reducing crop yields, leading to greater food insecurity.

Many diverse and underserved communities are disproportionately impacted by climate change and now face higher barriers to health and access to nutritious foods. And these same communities are most at risk for hidden hunger as well as obesity. For these reasons, one of the ways Kellogg is achieving their *Better Days Promise* is by feeding 375 million people in need through food donations and supporting children through feeding programs by the end of 2030.

For these reasons, Kellogg has aligned with the United Nations Sustainable Development Goal (SDG) #2—Zero Hunger—and is collaborating with others around the world to do their part to help "end hunger, achieve food security and improved nutrition, and promote sustainable agriculture by the end of 2030."[6]

AARP is another good example of how organizations are implementing one of the SDG goals that aligns with their mission. They have aligned with the United Nations SDG #3—Good Health and Well-Being. I am so proud of my friend and colleague, Margot James Copeland, a former Corporate Executive and current AARP board member who is passionate about this goal and is speaking out on behalf of the underserved communities for a greater focus on disparities in health care.

Once companies identify their CSR goals, they need a plan in place to measure it. What are the specific actions that can be implemented to achieve these goals and for it to be sustainable? This is where business sustainability comes in. Companies measure the results of their corporate social responsibility (CSR) goals in three ways:

E – Environment, how a company will protect ecology and the environment

S – Social, a company's policies to support human rights

G – Corporate Governance, the management and operation of the company and its decision makers[7]

These are the three specific actions a company can take to achieve their Corporate Social Responsibility (CSR) goals and is commonly known as **ESG.**

If you are passionate about any of your company's Corporate Social Responsibility goals, review your company's website or contact Human Resources to find out what sustainability goals they support and how to get involved. If you are interested in other SDGs that are not a part of your company's CSR goals, contact a national nonprofit organization, like United Way. Use the seventeen SDGs as a guide to decide which sustainable project you would like to volunteer for.

In addition to setting goals to achieve the company's CSR goals, companies are making it easier to volunteer. In spite of my desire to volunteer and the joy that I get from doing so, there has always been one barrier in particular that prevented me from doing it more often. The demands of my business and home often limited me from getting involved more and giving back as often as I would have liked to.

Many others face this same obstacle. To ensure their workers have time to volunteer, employers can help by offering:

- **Flexible scheduling**, such as flexible hours, compressed work weeks, or telecommuting options. This would enable employees to adjust their schedules and make time for volunteering activities without sacrificing their work commitments.

- **Paid volunteer time off**, specifically for volunteer work. This means employees would not have to use their vacation time or personal days for volunteering, which could make it easier for them to find the time to volunteer.

- **Volunteer opportunities during work hours or on company premises**. This would enable employees to participate in volunteer work without having to travel or take additional time off work. Additionally, it can help build a sense of community and teamwork among employees.

CHAPTER FOURTEEN

How You Can Make a Difference

When you know clearly what you want,
you wake up every morning excited about life.
—Mark Victor Hansen

Volunteering is a mutually beneficial activity that positively impacts everyone involved, including the volunteers, recipients, community, nonprofit organizations, and companies. Volunteers often feel a sense of satisfaction and fulfillment, which can lead to improved physical and emotional health and an enhanced sense of well-being. This, in turn, can result in more productive and collaborative employees and supportive family members. Employers who support volunteer efforts can earn the respect and appreciation of their employees. By participating in volunteer work, individuals can make a significant impact in their communities and beyond.

Shannon Loecher of UnitedHealthcare Social Responsibility discussed the difference they are making through their volunteer program, Do Good. Live Well.

"We consistently hear from individuals that 'we didn't think anyone cared,'" she said. "It's in that moment when I realize when you do something good for someone else, it really does make you feel good."[8]

I have found the same to be true for me. Whenever I volunteer, I feel fulfilled to know I'm giving back. When I hear of the difference I am making in a particular program, it fuels me to work even harder and leaves me immensely happy to be helping others in their time of need.

How to Get Started

Finding the right volunteer opportunity is important. You want to find something that matches your interests, personality, and expertise, as it will drive you and leave you with greater satisfaction. There are a wide variety of volunteer opportunities in every community. Whether you are interested in serving causes for youth, the environment, health, religion, or community, you'll have many choices available to you. Check with local nonprofit and cultural organizations, schools, faith communities, or hospitals for options.[9]

There are many different ways to get started. You can hear about volunteer opportunities by word of mouth, through your company, or even by Googling non-profit organizations. If your company has a Corporate Social Responsibility (CSR) group that focuses on giving back, you can contact them. The CSR groups within the company are aligned with the company's profit and purpose. If your company does not have a CSR group, you can go directly to the non-profit organization that you'd like to volunteer with.

If your company has a corporate commitment, this may serve as an entry point for you to get started. Depending on the opportunity, volunteering through your company may serve as a place where you can grow and professionally develop your skills. You may want to go out into the community and help by working with people or become a board member to impact the direction that the non-profit goes. You can also contact your local Chamber of Commerce, AmeriCorps, or seek out a Corporate Volunteer Council to serve on.

When you volunteer through your company, they have already done the research and know the non-profit organizations they work with are respectable, approved, and vested organizations worth donating to or volunteering. These organizations build volunteer experience programs so that volunteering is an experience for both you and the non-profit that you volunteer to help.

To determine where you should volunteer and in what capacity you'd like to serve, think about what you care about and what kind of legacy you want to leave in this world.

Company Volunteering

So, how do you begin to get involved through your company? Contact your Human Resources department to find out what is available and how it works. Ask them:

- Does your company have a volunteer program? If so, how does it work?

- What are your company's CSR goals (food insecurity, education, etc.)?

- Do they have a volunteer time off (VTO) policy? A VTO policy allows employees to take time off to volunteer during working hours without impacting their vacation time.

I am a perfect example of the impact these programs make in people's lives. One of my college professors was a part of IBM's VTO policy and recommended me as a student candidate. I ended up being interviewed by IBM and then hired. This professor and IBM's volunteer program changed my life forever. You, too, can make a difference in the lives of others this way.

Individual Volunteering

If you decide to volunteer on an individual basis, you'll want to find a reputable non-profit organization. Do your research to learn more about them by asking people who serve them already or are familiar with them or by Googling the company. You may even learn about the non-profit organization by word of mouth from others in your company or through your community.

If you already know the non-profit at which you want to serve, simply contact them to see what openings they have available and how you can join. Non-profit organizations are often looking for additional help and will be glad to bring you on board.

United Way, for example, is always looking for help and has information listed on their website about volunteering. You can find your local organization by searching online for "United Way of [insert your city]." Or, you can contact other non-profit organizations. Your local Chamber of Commerce is another good resource to contact.

One thing that I always liked about United Way is that they started every project I was involved in by sharing why they were doing that particular project. They wanted to educate the volunteers so they would understand the impact that we are having on the recipients.

Endless Opportunities

As you can see, there are endless opportunities when it comes to volunteering. Whatever you are passionate about, there is sure to be some nonprofit that needs your help. Don't be afraid to try something new or different. The benefits of volunteering are far too great to sit back and not get involved in your community. Take the time today to decide what you are passionate about, then contact the appropriate people to begin serving others and making an impact in the world.

> The benefits of volunteering are far too great to sit back and not get involved in your community.

SECTION FOUR
KEY TAKEAWAYS

1. A leader who becomes involved in the local community not only broadens personal leadership skills but also generates favorable public relations for your business or organization.

2. Volunteering gives you a sense of purpose, widens your network, shares your expertise, helps you grow as a leader, and benefits your physical and mental health.

3. Finding the right volunteer opportunity is important; it should be something that matches your interests, personality, and expertise, as it will drive you and leave you with greater satisfaction.

SECTION FIVE
IT'S ABOUT SELF-CARE

*Self-care is critical for maintaining the physical and
mental health required to be a great leader.*
—Carla A. Harris

It was the day before Thanksgiving. I always looked forward to my mom coming to visit, and she was finally here, sitting at the kitchen island, giving me a "mother talk." I remember it as clearly as if it were yesterday.

"Jacquline," she said, (she was the only person in the world who called me by my given name!) "I have watched you all week. You work non-stop. I may not know what you are doing, but I do know that you can't continue at this pace before you burn yourself out."

That was the first time I ever heard someone mention burnout. At that point, I didn't really know what burnout felt like. All I knew was that I had become consumed with doing everything flawlessly, 100% of the time.

Growing up during the Civil Rights Movement as African Americans, we were always told we weren't "good enough" simply because of the color of our skin. I had to constantly prove myself. In corporate America, I had to do the same. I was always being questioned and always had a more difficult time getting my ideas accepted. It was not easy without company assigned mentors or sponsors, but somehow I had gotten to an advanced career level without mentors or sponsors, unlike my White counterparts. I had great performance ratings, but I never received the support that my White peers had.

As I began to think about what my mother was saying, I questioned if I was actually in a burnout state. And, if I was, how could I be "normal" again? I had been functioning like this for so long that it had become my normal.

I wasn't sure if Mom was right, but I did know that life wasn't fun anymore. I felt like I was living to work rather than working to live. I was chronically exhausted and overwhelmed with a mountain of to-dos on my list. The more to-dos I completed, the more there was to do. I was always falling behind with the tasks and felt like I had no control. As a result, I worked non-stop. I slept about four hours a night, finding it more and more difficult to get up each morning. I was tired all the time. I prided myself on being able to juggle many things at once, but it became more and more difficult to do that.

My ability to perform my job was getting harder and harder. My productivity was taking a hit. I found myself up late at night after putting my son to bed, trying to complete tasks that I normally could do in a few hours. Because I had a reputation for getting things done, my manager often gave me lots of responsibilities. But when you are a perfectionist, this can be a slippery slope. What we know today is that burnout particularly affects people who are conscientious, committed, and deeply passionate about their work. Mokokoma Mokhonoana said, "The wise strive for the best. The foolish strive for perfection." What do you strive for?

Studies show that two of the major causes of burnout are a hostile workplace environment and being treated unfairly. As I write this book, I am able to clearly reflect back to that time and see I was experiencing major burnout. It was probably the worst experience in my professional career.

CHAPTER FIFTEEN

Workplace Stress Leads to Burnout

There will always be someone who can't see your worth.
Don't let it be you.
—Mel Robbins

My manager, Chuck, my peer managers, and I were waiting on an announcement to find out the division's new president. Though we were a team of superstars who achieved our revenue targets year after year, we were a little on edge, not knowing what new changes lie ahead. Then, Jim was named our new leader. None of us knew him, but his credentials were stellar.

After about thirty days, Jim announced his plans for a reorganization. He was bringing in his own cronies to replace most of the current team leaders, including me. If we wanted to keep our job, we had to interview for it. We were all in shock.

No problem, we thought. *Why wouldn't we be the best candidates? After all, our leadership team has achieved over 100%*

of our revenue targets year after year. We are the cash cows of the organization.

Barry, a White sales rep who supported my team, told me he had gone out to dinner with Jim a few weeks prior and was assured that he would be safe. *How interesting,* I thought, *since Barry said he didn't know Jim when he was announced as the Division's president.*

It wasn't long after that when the announcement came that Barry had been named to take over my role. Barry was the first person to call me. He wanted me to know he was embarrassed because he didn't realize that he would be taking my job. He apologized, then told me not to worry. He said he would hire me because he couldn't run my team. I realized that since I did not look like Jim or Barry, I needed to find another job outside of the division. I began to look feverishly.

I found myself coming to work each day in panic mode. *Would I have a job? Would I be fired?* This anxiety took its toll on me.

The next announcement was that another White manager was going to replace Betsy, one of the most experienced leaders in our group. She wasn't the right color, either. My manager, Chuck, a man of color, was also told he was losing his current position, but he would have a position in the organization. It turned out he was being moved to a lower-level job.

One day, Chuck came to each of his direct reports and told us he was going to Corporate HR to file a formal complaint, and if we wanted to be a part of it, we could, but there was no pressure to join him. My immediate response was, "I'm with you."

We were positive we would prevail. We had so much evidence to justify unfair treatment and discrimination. Within six months, all of my peer managers, who were people of color, had been relocated to other divisions. After two years of HR investigating the complaint, the findings were not in our favor. They said some of the responsibilities in our *original* job description were different from *the new* job description, so essentially it was not the same job.

By the time the findings were released, I was in a different job within the organization. But even if I had been fired, I knew it was more important to stand up and fight for what was right than to be demoted. I hear so many stories from clients about how the "system" changes the rules, processes, or guidelines so it comes out on top, rather than truly being fair to the employees. What's important to know if you find yourself in a situation like this is that you are not alone. There are other people of color experiencing the same challenges.

A Growing Concern

The term "burnout" was coined in 1974 by Herbert Freudenberger.[1] In 2019, the World Health Organization (WHO) classified it as a medical diagnosis, describing burnout as "a syndrome conceptualized as resulting from chronic workplace stress that has not been successfully managed."[2] A *Harvard Business Review* article describes burnout as "the mental and physical exhaustion you experience when the demands of your work consistently exceed the amount of energy you have available...(it) has been called the epidemic of the modern workplace."[3]

Employees and leaders are increasingly reporting being burned out at work. In a recent "Women in the Workplace" survey by McKinsey & Company, more than a third feel like they are expected to be "always on." Of those, 57% are burned out. A culture of always being on is not productive for the organization.

A significant 84% percent of HR directors either *agree* or *strongly agree* that burnout is an issue that needs to be addressed in their organization.[4] And employees and leaders are increasingly reporting feeling burned out at work, with

- 89% of employees saying they experienced burnout during the past year,[5]
- 60% of leaders feeling "used up" at work,[6] and
- 53% of workers reporting feeling burned out on a daily or weekly basis.

However, not everyone experiences burnout the same way. The same McKinsey & Company survey shows 42% of women feel burned out compared to 35% of men. And people of color are at a higher risk of burnout, with 36% of Black, Indigenous, and people of color (BIPOC) reporting feelings of exhaustion and hopelessness compared to only 26% of White respondents.[7]

Burnout has a significant impact on an organization's bottom line and employee health. Increased turnover, absenteeism, disengagement, and reduced performance are just a few of the ways burnout impacts an organization. The costs to employee health often result in complications in physical and mental health and increased mortality.

Burnout has a significant impact on an organization's bottom line and employee health.

To create a culture where employees can do their best work with less risk of burnout, leaders and managers need to understand the root causes of burnout. One recent survey cites six core domains that lead to burnout within organizations.

- Workload. Is the complexity of the work tasks and processes adequate for all?

- Role Clarity and Autonomy. Do you understand the job responsibilities, have control over how the work is completed, and feel you have the adequate resources (e.g., training, mentor, sponsor) to be successful?

- Supervisor and Co-worker Relationships. Is there bi-directional communication and cooperation?

- Rewards and Recognition. Are there monetary and non-monetary rewards?

- Fairness and Equity. Are the organizational processes and policies (e.g., work assignments, promotions, pay increases) fair?

- Employee and Organizational Values. Are the employee values in alignment with the organization?[8]

Burnout can manifest itself in many ways, including anxiety, depression, insomnia, IBS, asthma, panic attacks, anxiety, heart palpitations, irritability, skin breakouts–pretty much anything which gets worse with stress, which is…everything. In addition to the three byproducts of burnout that Christina Maslach found in her research–exhaustion, negativity, and poor performance–there is likely a pattern or sign that is uniquely yours alone.[9]

Signs of burnout manifest themselves in three categories: physical, emotional, and behavioral. Patterns that indicate burnout can include:

- Having more bad days than good
- Feeling exhausted constantly
- Frequent illnesses
- No longer being excited or challenged by your work
- Blunted emotions
- Lack of motivation
- Feeling unrecognized and undervalued[10]

If any of these are what you're feeling, you may need to evaluate areas in your life that are causing the stress. And when you discover your particular symptoms, you can use them as a guiding tool to help you stay on track and prevent burnout.

Burnout Among Women of Color

Many women of color are breadwinners in their families and are motivated to get that next raise, promotion, or bonus, so they often work 60-80 hours per week. This is the only way they know how to prove their worth. It's hard to prioritize our mental health when it feels like our jobs and success are on the line, especially when we have been told our whole lives that we have to work twice as hard to get the same opportunities. Over half of Black women feel their ethnicity or race will make it harder to get a raise or promotion. There are always unwritten and unknown-to-us rules that are brought up when it's time to get a raise or promotion.[11]

But it's important to know that you have to advocate for yourself. *You* are your own best cheerleader. Growing up, we were told to just do our jobs and we would be recognized for it, but in corporate America, that is not the case. I learned that early in my sales position.

One way I was successful in advocating for myself was by getting client feedback. The first time I received feedback was after I had successfully helped clients install their software. I asked my client how he would rate the installation. He said that it was a "10 out of 10," so I asked him if he would communicate his satisfaction with the installation to my management team. After he did, I finally received recognition at our monthly sales meeting.

When advocating for yourself doesn't work and you have exhausted getting any resolution from the decision-making process within your organization, you can always take it to the EEOC, a federal agency that handles equal opportunity cases; just be sure you are well-armed with all of the specific details and facts around the case.

A recent Mental Health Match article discusses some key reasons why women of color are at risk for burnout:[12]

1. We are conditioned to put our needs last, taking care of everyone at work and at home first and often neglecting to nurture our own needs.

2. We lack mentors and sponsors to support our leadership journey and don't get promotions while being told that we are doing a great job.

3. We face systematic career advancement and growth barriers—49% of Black women feel their ethnicity or race will make it harder to get a raise/promotion compared to 11% of women overall. In 2022, women of color represented 19% of entry-level positions. Very few advanced to leadership positions: managers (14%) senior managers/directors (10%), VPs (8%), SVPs (6%), and C-suite positions (5%).[13]

4. We have to go "above and beyond" to be seen as equal while being overworked and underpaid. Excessive demands when you know that your work isn't valued in the same way as your peers can bring about cynicism and detachment.

5. We are often subject to external thoughts and expressions in the form of microaggressions, which can be exhausting and impact our self-worth and identity. We also deal with hostile environments which include stereotypes (that we are angry, incompetent, and/or intellectually inferior, constantly under a microscope), rudeness, racial jokes or insensitivity, and being ignored and/or harassed.

6. We feel we have to represent our entire race at work. We are asked culturally specific questions. People comment on how articulately we speak, or ask if they can touch our hair, or even pose the question, "What is keeping the Black community down?"

These types of issues have to be dealt with daily and can cause anxiety, depression, or other medical issues (such as upset stomach, increased blood pressure, chest pain, insomnia, and frequent colds due to a compromised immune system).

When you are doing all the right things to advance, but the opposing forces are pushing you down, it is clear how the burnout signals of exhaustion, cynicism, and detachment can make you feel there is no way to get ahead.

Our Own Role in Burnout

Burnout can also be something we bring upon ourselves. We feel the need to chase that unattainable perfection in all areas of our lives, charging full steam ahead, certain that if we just work harder or longer, we'll reach our idea of excellence.

We push ourselves at work to take on more tasks and work long hours so we can feel we did our part and are being an outstanding worker. After working those long hours, we come home and begin to scrub, organize, and decorate our home so it will look just like the impeccable dream house we saw in a Southern Living magazine or on our Pinterest board. But we must do so as expeditiously as possible, because we can't forget about our family.

We must also be the perfect wife and mom. Our family needs us, both collectively and individually, so we carve out time with our kids to play and read with them, chauffeur them to friends' houses, and attend every sports game. We listen to our partner recount their day and make sure they have time to spend on their hobbies.

As if that's not all, we feel the pressure to be involved anywhere that needs help. Church needs assistance? Sure, we'll volunteer! School needs another parental chaperone for a field trip or snacks for a party? Sign us up!

No matter what it is, we push ourselves to be everywhere and do everything to ensure the needs of everyone around us are met. But there are only so many hours in the day, and we only have so much energy. There will come a point where we burn out, unable to keep going and realizing the illusion that perfection is.

CHAPTER SIXTEEN

Self-Care Coping Strategies

Who looks outside, dreams. Who looks inside, awakes.
—Carl Jung

The Journal of Black Studies' review, "Black Women Talk About Workplace Stress and How they Cope," indicates that, "African American women use emotion- and problem-focused coping responses to manage stress (e.g. racism and sexism) in the workplace."

- They change the way they think or the expectations they have for themselves.

- They adjust the way they act in one context after another.

- They try to cover up their intelligence with one group of friends and do everything possible to prove it to another.

- They deny their sadness and loneliness.[14]

It is unfortunate that we have felt the need to resort to coping strategies like these which often result in burnout, especially when there are better ways to cope. Let's take a look at some recommended ways to manage stress and reduce the likelihood of burnout:

Taking breaks often. Just stepping away for twenty-minute breaks helps. Add this to your calendar as if it were a client meeting.

Practicing resilience. Set boundaries and practice resilience. Resilience is about how you recharge, not how you endure. Once I began to work from home, there was not a clear separation between my work and home life. When I wasn't sitting in front of the laptop, I was thinking about how to resolve a problem. Then, I'd find myself hopping on the laptop to send a quick email. I had become a "workaholic." If you are trying to build resilience at work, you need adequate internal and external recovery periods where you unplug; one way to do this is to not have lunch at your desk.[15]

Taking all of your paid time off (PTO). You've earned it, so use it! I used to feel that I couldn't take time off because my workload would double. But guess what? The workload doesn't go away even if you don't take PTO. It's important to keep that perspective in mind and manage the workload versus letting it manage you.

Speaking up when you need help and support. Communicate your workload to your manager and what has priority, then get those things done. Your manager may not be aware of how overwhelmed you feel. If everything has priority, ask for an assistant to help or for another team member to pick those tasks up. You're probably thinking you will never get promoted if you ask for help, but if you have a good relationship with your manager where there is trust and support, this will not keep you from getting promoted.

Prioritizing self-care. Anything that invigorates you and makes you feel alive again is a must. Make time for self-care strategies such as working out, pampering yourself (massage, nails, sauna, long baths), walking, quiet time, and reflecting. Find a hobby that calms and balances. (For me, it's yoga and pilates.) Participate in other activities like painting, ceramics, book club and even dancing. If you enjoy playing cards, have a card party. Explore outdoor activities that re-energize you with the fresh air like walking in the park, riding your bike, or hiking. These social activities could even help to expand your professional network while restoring your inner self.

Building a community of supportive women. Join organizations where you can develop friendships and professional relationships with talented and like-minded women of color. Girlfriends have really helped my sanity. During my life, I have been surrounded by supportive women. My high school, college, sorority, and professional Sistas have been there for me and have helped to carry me over when I needed support. Most of them work in similar business environments and share experiences similar to mine. Going out to dinner or for drinks to reconnect with friends and just laughing helps to relieve my stress. A colleague once told me that his dad often said, "A day without laughter is a day without sunshine."

Building an infrastructure support system. Integrating work and home can be a stressful juggling act. It definitely creates skills in multitasking and prioritizing what needs to get done, but it can also make you realize you're not a superwoman. I came to that realization myself and knew I needed help. I learned a lot from my friend Beverly, who had two kids, was a school principal, was active in her church and several other social organizations, and even took on leadership roles within those organizations. I could not figure out how she was able to juggle things so well, but as I observed her, I found that she would make friends with the parents who her children played with. They could then collectively shoulder tasks for the kids, taking turns picking them up after school and babysitting and such. No one can do all of this without a support system. We all need people who can help, listen, and share their experiences with us. And, for both men and women, it takes a support network to help build a long-term successful career.

Leaning into your faith. Prayer, church, meditation, and community involvement are so beneficial to self-care. My prayer for you is that you have a higher power that guides you and helps you through trials and tribulations.

Volunteering. Serve others by helping with activities that you enjoy. Giving back and bringing joy to others may help you feel needed and appreciated.

Finding a therapist. This has been an invaluable resource for me. When my dad died on my birthday in my early 30s, I could not believe he was gone at such a young age. I sought a therapist to talk with, and it was incredibly helpful in helping me sort through my thoughts and emotions. A few years ago, I facilitated a few sessions for a Fortune 500 company whose employee survey feedback indicated the company did not support women or African Americans. In one of my focus groups, a Black lady spoke up immediately. She was the only C-Suite executive of color and said if it hadn't been for her therapist, she would not be there. This honesty and openness spoke to the participants. When looking for a therapist, be sure to interview them to make sure they are a good match for you. You can even go in person or meet online. Look at your options, and find what works best for you.

Exploring music. Uncover a calming app or music that relaxes you.

Changing course. And finally, there is always the option to do what former Atlanta Mayor Keisha Lance Bottoms did. After the height of the pandemic, the 2020 riots, a major cyberattack, and a federal investigation into corruption under her predecessor, Bottoms announced that she would not run for re-election in 2022. She admitted that being mayor was never a great fit for her personality, describing herself as "an introvert masking as an extrovert" and someone who would "much rather be somewhere reading a book than sitting at a party."[16] Sometimes, when we are in the wrong job, we need to just walk away for our own sanity. Remember, just like "it takes a village to raise a child," it takes a village to support you through your leadership journey. Don't go at it alone. Reach out to others for support. As an old African Proverb says, "If you want to go fast, go alone; if you want to go far, go together."

How Leaders Can Address Burnout

Leaders in organizations can foster positive, burnout-mitigating employee experiences by ensuring that employees feel supported. They can invest in their employees by periodically checking in and:

- Listening to work-related problems.

- Encouraging teamwork, ensuring everyone's opinion counts.

- Assigning work that is purposeful and manageable.

- Placing performance expectations and metrics within employees' control, and focusing on strengths-based feedback and development.

- Designing jobs to allow for autonomy.

- Providing collaboration spaces that are inviting.

Addressing burnout on an organizational level may require working with HR to make it a company-wide initiative. McLean & Company suggests following its three-step plan:

1. **Identify root causes of burnout:** Determine key roles and responsibilities in evaluating and addressing burnout. This includes gathering existing internal data to assess the current state of burnout, using a questionnaire to gather the data, then identifying the high-priority groups. Focus groups are a good way to capture the employees' needs and identify priority root causes of burnout. Determining goals and metrics are also critical.

2. **Tailor solutions to address root causes of burnout:** Explore solutions across the six burnout domains. Create a shortlist based on employee needs and organizational resourcing constraints. Identify and consult with stakeholders to finalize a list of solutions. Create a roadmap to outline solution implementation and plan for the change management process.

3. **Create a future with minimal burnout:** Revise organizational policies and programs to identify gaps and opportunities for minimizing burnout. Provide tools and training for managers to help them identify and minimize burnout within their teams. Develop a communication plan to promote solution uptake. And,

finally, create a plan to reevaluate and monitor organizational burnout.[17]

Assessing burnout requires ongoing effort, not a one-time task. Continuous evaluation and adjustment of solutions are necessary as triggers and signs of burnout persistently emerge.

SECTION FIVE
KEY TAKEAWAYS

1. Burnout has a significant impact on an organization's bottom line and employee health, such as increased turnover, absenteeism, disengagement, and reduced performance.

2. Signs of burnout manifest themselves in three categories: physical, emotional, and behavioral.

3. Leaders in organizations can foster positive, burnout-mitigating employee experiences by ensuring that employees feel supported.

4. Assessing burnout is an ongoing process, not a one-time effort. Triggers and signs of burnout will continuously surface, creating the need for continuous reevaluation and adjustment of solutions.

5. It takes a village to support you through your leadership journey. Don't go it alone. Reach out to others for support.

ACKNOWLEDGMENTS

Well, here we are at the end of this book. It is a bittersweet moment for me. This book is dedicated to my parents and my brother, Ron. They were my role models. They were always so sure of their purpose in life. I, on the other hand, grew up not quite sure of my purpose.

My mother and father were also my mentors. I watched and became energized as they strategized how to "get around the mountains" in their lives. My mom, Mary, was an English teacher. She said she always loved reading and writing, so she knew she wanted to be a teacher.

When you walked into her office at home, she had books by authors from all over the world. She learned about other countries and cultures by reading. Had she been born during a different time, she would have been a famous journalist. I watched my mother apply to graduate school at the University of South Carolina with a 3.5 GPA and receive a rejection letter saying that she did not meet their requirements.

But she did not let that stop her. She applied to an Ivy League school, Columbia University, and was accepted into their graduate program. Her acceptance letter said they were honored to have her in their program. Each summer, when school was out, my mother packed us up and we headed from South Carolina to New York City, where my mother attended classes.

During that time, we couldn't eat in restaurants, so our car smelled like fried chicken and potato salad, but we loved the smell because we were so excited to be going to New York. My mom taught me that no one defines your destiny.

My dad, a Baptist minister warmly known as "Rev," said he always knew he would be a preacher. He pastored two churches and worked at a local HBCU college. In 2013, twenty-five years after he died, he was still remembered and inducted into his college's hall of fame. So many students came back to talk about how he influenced their lives.

He would sometimes come with us to New York and attend the graduate seminary school at Columbia University. His sermons shaped me Sunday after Sunday. Each time something or someone stood in my way, I thought of my dad, standing in the pulpit, wearing his big white robe, smiling out at the congregation, ending his Sunday sermons:

> *When you go down the road and you run into a mountain, I said... when you run into a mountain, if you can't go through the mountain, look to your right, look to your left, look over the mountain, look under the mountain—because there is always a way around the mountain.*

When I would say, "I can't do it, Dad," he would say, "There is no such word as can't. Go back and try it again."

And there's my big brother, Ron. He was my protector. He was always there to help me. He always knew he wanted to be a doctor to help others. He and I had this sibling rivalry as to who would be the first to tell their story.

Ron's story was so powerful. He was the first Black person to graduate from the University of South Carolina School of Pharmacy. He told me how they treated him and that he should have graduated first instead of second in his class, but he remained resilient and persevered.

He served our country as a Lt. Colonel in the United States Army and went on to become one of the first Black surgical oncologists in the world. In his city, Augusta, Georgia, he was well-known and respected in his private practice. He received the key to the city, and a day was officially named after him.

Sadly, he succumbed to the very disease he cured in so many others and passed away on December 26, 2019. The United States House of Representatives honored him in 2020, and he was officially put in the United States history books. He was my hero. I am sad that his story will never be told and that he will never get to read his little sister's story and my way of "giving back."

And, then there was me, "Jackie." I never knew what I wanted to be. During my time, most girls were encouraged to be teachers or major in liberal arts. My parents never encouraged me to do that. They always said, *Do what you enjoy—as long as you can make a living doing it.*

I knew what they meant. I was like my brother and drawn to the sciences and math. Today, we know it as STEM degrees—science, technology, engineering, and math.

What I have learned is if you take one step, God will help you take the next step. I was asked how long I have been working on this book. When I responded, probably ten years, I was asked, "What took you so long?"

When I started this book, so many obstacles stood in my way. In 2008, the stock market crashed, and I took a major loss. In 2010, the Gulf Shore oil spill happened in Florida, and suddenly all of my rental tenants were out of work and left the area. I lost those properties as people escaped Florida to find work.

I began seven years of a dark time in my life. During those years, while everyone was out partying on New Year's Eve, I was home praying that I would not lose another close relative. I lost my mother, my mother-in-law, my husband, my brother, my uncle, my aunt, and my best friend, Thom. All during that time, I imagined my father telling me, "There's a way around the mountain." The storm doesn't last forever, so don't look at the troubles you see now; rather, fix your gaze on things that cannot be seen. (2 Corinthians 4:17-18 NLT)

When I started this book, the "experts" told me that my leadership book had to be either a self-development book or a memoir, but both elements could not be in the same book. And, then I met some awesome editors, Bill, Jen, and the entire StoryBuilders team who believed in my vision.

There were many people who helped and supported me along the way, and it would be impossible to name them all here. However, I would like to acknowledge at least a few. My sister-in-law, Brenda, introduced me to Kimothy, who helped me craft the first two chapters of this book. And my Sista Beverly, a school principal, gave me feedback that helped get me through the first few chapters.

Linda and Thom were always there when I felt that this book process was too hard; they reminded me that there are women who needed to hear my message. My Sista girls, Loraine, Renee, Judi, Carol and Gloria, were there to cheer me on. And a special Sista thanks to Mona McClellan, aka TheBoomerBelle2723 (YouTube)—a friend and brilliant videographer—for all of her support. My niece, Sincerai and my goddaughters, Kim and Chandra, were always there to help. This is what I mean by when you take one step, God will help you take the next step.

I must thank my son, Michael Jamaal, for always being there to cheer me on. Love you, son!

Remember, we all go through challenging seasons in our lives. These are the moments that define us and give us opportunities to discover that we are capable of life-changing action and transformation. Just because the world says it has to be a certain way, does not mean that it actually has to be.

Be curious. Ask about the reason things are being done the way they are. Challenge the status quo. Try something different. This is how history is made.

I am honored that you picked this book to read. I hope you find some tools and strategies in this book to help you navigate around the mountains in your own life. As you continue on your journey, feel the fire, and keep moving forward.

The worst that can happen is that you fail. And, by the way, failure is just another learning experience. Learn from it, and come back stronger and more powerful.

But the best thing that can happen is that you *win*. You won't know if you don't take the chance. In the words of Marianne Williamson's, *A Return to Love: Reflections on the Principles of a Course in Miracles*:

> Our deepest fear is not that we are inadequate. Our deepest fear is that we are powerful beyond measure. It is our light, not our darkness, that most frightens us. Your playing small does not serve the world. We are all meant to shine.[1]

ABOUT THE AUTHOR

Jackie Stallings Evans, award-winning author, ICF Certified Leadership Coach, and BCC Certified Coach is a trailblazer in the world of leadership coaching and consulting, dedicated to propelling women into higher levels of corporate leadership. With a remarkable journey that spans from her humble beginnings in an entry-level role to becoming an executive at IBM, a Fortune 100 company, Jackie personifies the path she champions. Additionally, she acts as a mentor with the Rutgers University Center for Women in Business, further testament to her commitment to women's leadership. This comprehensive experience offers her clients—especially women aspiring to ascend the corporate ladder—a distinctive blend of empathy and expertise.

With over three decades of experience, Jackie has engaged with diverse industries, mastering the intricacies of driving results within teams and organizations. Her groundbreaking Rising Leader Model, shaped by real-world challenges and successes, equips female leaders with tools and strategies to navigate and advance in today's global marketplace.

Jackie's collaborations with industry leaders, such as IBM Corporation, Adobe, Ernst & Young, Kaiser Permanente, and Mastercard, underscore her impeccable reputation. Yet, it is her unwavering commitment to advancing women in leadership that truly sets her apart. As a trusted advisor, Jackie focuses on providing clients with effective and practical business solutions that deliver measurable results for their specific organizational challenges. Her passion lies in helping leaders to excel in today's volatile, uncertain, complex, and ambiguous (VUCA) world, recognizing that traditional leadership models don't work in this constantly changing and evolving landscape.

Jackie Stallings Evans is a visionary catalyst, passionate about empowering women leaders into higher realms of leadership.

Contact Jackie at info@jackiestallingsevans.com or visit her webpage at jackiestallingsevans.com.

NOTES

Chapter One

1. Jackson, Mahalia. "Lord Don't Move the Mountain." Accessed June 18, 2023. Lyrics.com, STANDS4 LLC, 2023. https://www.lyrics.com/lyric/8152005/Mahalia+Jackson/Lord+Don%26%23039%3Bt+Move+the+Mountain.

2. McGregor, Jena. "Walgreens' Vaccine Rollout Will Be Led by the Only Black Woman Helming a Fortune 500 Company." The Washington Post, September 2, 2021. https://www.washingtonpost.com/business/2021/01/29/walgreens-ceo-roz-brewer-black-fortune-500/.

3. LeanIn.Org, McKinsey & Company. "The State of Black Women in Corporate America." Lean In, 2020. https://leanin.org/research/state-of-black-women-in-corporate-america.

4. ibid

5. ibid

6. ibid

7. ibid

8. Ibid

9. LeanIn.Org, McKinsey & Company. "Women in the Workplace 2022: Key Findings & Takeaways." Lean In, 2022. https://leanin.org/women-in-the-workplace.

10. Ibid

11. LeanIn.Org, McKinsey & Company. "Women in the Workplace 2021: The Full Report." Lean In, 2021. https://leanin.org/women-in-the-workplace/2021/.

12. Obama, Michelle. "Michelle Obama Quote." AZQuotes.com, 2012. https://azquotes.com/quote/563763.

Chapter Two

1. "IBM Copyright and Trademark Information." IBM, 2023. https://www.ibm.com/legal/copytrade.

2. "Think (Slogan)." Wikipedia, May 12, 2023. https://en.wikipedia.org/wiki/Think_(slogan).

3. Harris, Carla A. *Lead to Win: How to Be a Powerful, Impactful, Influential Leader in Any Environment.* Avery Publishing, 2022, page 17.

4. Ward, Marguerite. "What Is a Microaggression? 15 Things People Think Are Fine to Say at Work - but Are Actually Racist, Sexist, or Offensive." Business Insider, February 15, 2023. https://www.businessinsider.com/microaggression-unconscious-bias-at-work-2018-6#oh-sorry-wrong-person-3.

5. LeanIn.Org, McKinsey & Company. "Women in the Workplace 2021: The Full Report." Lean In, 2021. https://leanin.org/women-in-the-workplace/2021/.

6. ibid

7. ibid

8. ibid

9. Aragão, Carolina. "Gender Pay Gap in U.S. Hasn't Changed Much in Two Decades." Pew Research Center, March 1, 2023. https://www.pewresearch.org/short-reads/2023/03/01/gender-pay-gap-facts/.

10. Patten, Eileen. "Racial, Gender Wage Gaps Persist in U.S. despite Some Progress." Pew Research Center, July 1, 2016. https://www.pewresearch.org/short-reads/2016/07/01/racial-gender-wage-gaps-persist-in-u-s-despite-some-progress/.

11. Quiroz-Gutierrez, Marco. "Why Black Women's Wage Gap Is a Problem for Everyone." Fortune, August 3, 2021. https://fortune.com/2021/08/03/black-women-equal-pay-day-2021-wage-gap-gender-race/.

12. Ibid

13. LeanIn.Org, McKinsey & Company. "Women in the Workplace 2022: Key Findings & Takeaways." Lean In, 2022. https://leanin.org/women-in-the-workplace.

14. ibid

15. Ashcraft, Catherine. "The Tricky (and Necessary) Business of Being a Male Advocate for Gender ..." fastcompany.com, May 28, 2015.

Section One

1. "Hampton University-2021 Main Commencement Ceremony." YouTube, May 9, 2021. https://www.youtube.com/watch?v=oFTwDvo50zA.

2. Schwarzer, Ralf, and Aleksandra Luszczynska. "Chapter Eleven: Self-Efficacy." Essay. In *Handbook of Positive Psychology Assessment*, 207–217. East York (Ont.), MA: Hogrefe, 2023.

3. ibid

4. Smallwood, Norm. "Define Your Personal Leadership Brand in Five Steps." Harvard Business Review, March 2, 2021. https://hbr.org/2010/03/define-your-personal-leadershi.

5. Miller, Jo. "Woman of Influence Resources." Jo Miller, December 3, 2021. https://jomiller.com/womanofinfluence/.

6. Harris, Carla A. *Lead to Win: How to Be a Powerful, Impactful, Influential Leader in Any Environment.* Avery Publishing, 2022, page 31.

7. Hill, Napoleon, and Arthur R. Pell. *Think and grow rich: The landmark bestseller--now revised and updated for the 21st Century.* New York, NY: Jeremy P. Tarcher/Penguin, 2014.

8. Goldsmith, Marshall, and Mark Reiter. *What got you here won't get you there: How successful people become even more successful!* New York, NY, NY: Hachette Go, an imprint of Hachette Books, 2020.

9. Somers, Meredith. "Women Are Less Likely than Men to Be Promoted. Here's One Reason Why." MIT Sloan, April 12, 2022. https://mitsloan.mit.edu/ideas-made-to-matter/women-are-less-likely-men-to-be-promoted-heres-one-reason-why.

10. ibid

11. Shue, Kelly. "Women Aren't Promoted Because Managers Underestimate Their Potential." Yale Insights, September 17, 2021. Accessed April 22, 2024. https://insights.som.yale.edu/insights/women-arent-promoted-because-managers-underestimate-their-potential

12. Williams, Joan C. *Bias interrupted: Creating inclusion for real and for good.* Cambridge, USA: Harvard Business Review Press, 2022.

13. Valentine, Gerry. "Council Post: Executive Presence: What Is It, Why You Need It and How to Get It." Forbes, October 12, 2022. https://www.forbes.com/

14. ibid

15. ibid

Section Two

1. Whitmore, John. *Coaching for performance*. Boston, MA: Nicholas Brealey, 2017.

2. ibid

Section Three

1. Unit, Economist Intelligence. Rep. *Skills Mismatch: Business Acumen and Strategy Execution*, 2015. chrome-extension://efaidnbmnn-nibpcajpcglclefindmkaj/https://btsspark.org/docs/white-papers/skills-mismatch-business-acumen-and-strategy-execution-research-C276E653B841.pdf?sfvrsn=2.

2. Schoemaker, Paul J.H., Steve Krupp, and Samantha Howland. "Strategic Leadership: The Essential Skills." Harvard Business Review, September 13, 2021. https://hbr.org/2013/01/strategic-leadership-the-esssential-skills.

3. Cote, Catherine. "Tips for Successful Strategy Formulation: HBS Online." Business Insights Blog, October 14, 2020. https://online.hbs.edu/blog/post/strategy-formulation.

4. Gerstner, Louis V. *Who says elephants can't dance?: Leading a great enterprise through dramatic change*. New York, NY: HarperBusiness, 2004.

5. "Simple Profit-Loss Statements and Templates - Indeed." indeed.com, 2023. https://www.indeed.com/hire/c/info/profit-loss-statement.

6. "Innovation, MS." Innovation, MS < Northeastern University, 2023. https://catalog.northeastern.edu/graduate/business/master-science/innovation-ms/.

7. ibid

8. ibid

9. Young, Swathi. "5 Key Benefits of Using a Business Model Canvas Instead of a Business Plan." Medium, April 11, 2018. https://chimera-swa.medium.com/5-key-benefits-of-using-a-business-model-canvas-instead-of-a-business-plan-55d5d727ba46.

10. Athuraliya, Amanda. "What Is a Business Model Canvas: Learn How to Create a Business Model Canvas with Examples." Creately, December 12, 2022. https://creately.com/guides/business-model-canvas-explained/

11. Alberdi, Raquel. "Business Model Canvas: A 9-Step Guide to Analyze Any Business." ThePower Business School, May 12, 2023. https://www.thepowermba.com/en/blog/business-model-canvas.

12. Valchev, Marin. "Business Acumen Skills & Competency: The Guide to Improving Them." Business Skills, Software and Knowledge You Truly Need, January 6, 2022. https://www.businessphrases.net/business-acumen/.

Section Four

1. UnitedHealthcare, VolunteerMatch. "Doing Good Is Good for You Study." unitedhealthgroup.com, 2017. https://www.unitedhealthgroup.com/content/dam/UHG/PDF/2013/UNH-Health-Volunteering-Study.pdf.

2. ibid

3. ibid

4. ibid

5. Lutkevich, Ben. "ESG vs. CSR vs. Sustainability: What's the Difference?" WhatIs.com, April 21, 2023. https://www.techtarget.com/whatis/feature/ESG-vs-CSR-vs-sustainability-Whats-the-difference.

6. Kellog's. "Better Days." Kellogg's Better Days, 2023. https://betterdays.kelloggcompany.com/.

7. West Editor, ibest. "What Are Sdgs, CSR, ESG? Do You Know the Differences?" Market Prospects, 2022. https://www.market-prospects.com/articles/what-are-sdgs-csr-esg.

8. UnitedHealthcare, VolunteerMatch. "Doing Good Is Good for You Study." unitedhealthgroup.com, 2017. https://www.unitedhealthgroup.com/content/dam/UHG/PDF/2013/UNH-Health-Volunteering-Study.pdf.

9. Angela Thoreson, L.I.C.S.W. "3 Health Benefits of Volunteering." Mayo Clinic Health System, August 25, 2022.

https://www.mayoclinichealthsystem.org/hometown-health/
speaking-of-health/3-health-benefits-of-volunteering.

Section Five

1. Heinemann, Linda V., and Torsten Heinemann. "Burnout Research." *SAGE Open* 7, no. 1 (January 2017): 2–2. https://doi.org/10.1177/2158244017697154.

2. "Burn-out an 'Occupational Phenomenon': International Classification of Diseases." World Health Organization, May 28, 2019. https://www.who.int/news/item/28-05-2019-burn-out-an-occupational-phenomenon-international-classification-of-diseases.

3. Knight, Rebecca. "How to Overcome Burnout and Stay Motivated." Harvard Business Review, April 2, 2015. https://hbr.org/2015/04/how-to-overcome-burnout-and-stay-motivated.

4. McLean & Company, McKinsey & Company, HR Plan to Extinguish Burnout, 2021

5. Visier. "The Burnout Epidemic Report 2021." Visier, 2021. https://www.visier.com/lp/burnout-epidemic-report-2021/.

6. McLean & Company, SHRM, HR Plan to Extinguish Burnout, 2021

7. McLean & Company, Extinguish Organizational Burnout, Accessed June 18, 2023.

8. ibid

9. Donovan, Caitlin. *The bouncebackability factor: End burnout, gain resilience, change the world.* New York, NY: Cait Donovan LLC , 2020.

10. Herrity, Jennifer. "9 Causes of Burnout (with Helpful Ways to Manage It) - Indeed." Indeed.com, February 3, 2023. https://www.indeed.com/career-advice/career-development/causes-of-burnout.

11. Byrd, Latesha. "5 Ways Women of Color Can Prioritize Their Well-Being at Work." The Muse, February 27, 2023. https://www.themuse.com/advice/women-of-color-prioritize-mental-health-wellbeing-work-career.

12. Crosby, Natasha. "How Women of Color Can Beat Burnout." Mental Health Match, May 10, 2021. https://mentalhealthmatch.com/articles/black-mental-health/women-of-color-beat-burnout.

13. LeanIn.Org, McKinsey & Company. "Women in the Workplace 2022: Key Findings & Takeaways." Lean In, 2022. https://leanin.org/women-in-the-workplace.

14. Hall, J. Camille, Joyce E. Everett, and Johnnie Hamilton-Mason. "Black Women Talk about Workplace Stress and How They Cope." *Journal of Black Studies* 43, no. 2 (2011): 207–26. https://doi.org/10.1177/0021934711413272.

15. Achor, Shawn, and Michelle Gielan. "Resilience Is About How You Recharge, Not How You Endure." Harvard Business Review, January 19, 2023. https://hbr.org/2016/06/resilience-is-about-how-you-recharge-not-how-you-endure.

16. Cheney-Rice, Zak. "Why Did Keisha Lance Bottoms Quit?" Intelligencer, January 3, 2022. https://nymag.com/intelligencer/2022/01/keisha-lance-bottoms-atlanta-mayor-quits.html.

17. Organizations Must Address Employee Burnout to Survive in the Post-Pandemic Future, 2022

Acknowledgments

1. Williamson, Marianne. *A return to love: Reflections on the principles of a course in miracles*. New York, NY: HarperOne, 2012.

www.ingramcontent.com/pod-product-compliance
Lightning Source LLC
LaVergne TN
LVHW022131210325
806549LV00001B/137